# Developing Media Skills

## Geoff Barton

**Heinemann**

Heinemann Educational Publishers
Halley Court, Jordan Hill, Oxford, OX2 8EJ
A division of Reed Educational & Professional Publishing Ltd
Heinemann is a registered trademark of Reed Educational &
Professional Publishing Ltd

OXFORD MELBOURNE AUCKLAND
JOHANNESBURG BLANTYRE GABORONE
IBADAN PORTSMOUTH NH (USA) CHICAGO

© Geoff Barton, 2001

First published 2001
ISBN 0 435 10960 X
05 04 03 02 01
10 9 8 7 6 5 4 3 2

Original illustrations © Heinemann Educational Publishers, 2001

**Illustrations**
Gecko DTP: page 9; Phil Healey, page 18; Martin Ursell, pages 22 and 23;
Alice Englander, page 34 and 35; Tim Davies, pages 38 and 43; Nick Schon,
page 48; Gecko DTP, pages 91–95.

Produced by Gecko Ltd, Bicester, Oxon
Cover design by Bigtop
Printed and bound in Spain by Mateo Cromo.

Picture research by Charlotte Lippmann

Tel: 01865 888058 www.heinemann.co.uk

# Introduction for teachers

*Developing Media Skills* has been written in response to the increased emphasis on media forms in the National Curriculum for English and the *Framework for Teaching English*, years 7–9. Most English teachers have placed a healthy emphasis on teaching about the media, but apart from newspapers, magazines and leaflets, obtaining suitable resources can be a challenge.

This book aims to provide you with a range of new **resources**. Some of them are the kinds of texts used within the media industry and are therefore particularly useful in exploring media processes.

The book also aims to build students' media skills. These are based on National Curriculum requirements. National Curriculum aims for each unit are outlined on our website (see below). It is important to stress that this is not a specialist media studies course book: it is designed to improve students' understanding of media forms within English.

The **skills** are clearly signalled to students at the start of each new section. They are drawn from the *Framework for Teaching English* and therefore should help in your planning of coverage of that document. For full coverage of the *Framework* objectives, a matching chart can be found on page 126.

The **organisation** of the book is very simple. We have chosen to focus on five major media forms, with opportunities for comparison between them in the final unit. Each unit has specific sections which lead up to extended assignments. You can therefore build small or larger parts of the book into your departmental schemes of work.

## Website activities

On our website you will find free downloadable resources to support you in using *Developing Media Skills*. The site contains customisable photocopiable worksheets that can be used:

• to support activities in the student book
• for homework.

Each unit is supported by 4–6 worksheets that can be downloaded from www.heinemann.co.uk/devmediaskills.

The **W** symbols in each unit indicate which activities are supported by our website.

I hope that the book – and the website – leads to plenty of lively media work in your classroom.

*Geoff Barton*

# Contents

**Introduction for teachers**     3
**Introduction for students**     7

## Unit One | Film    8

1.1 Messages through images    8
1.2 Sequencing images    15
1.3 Exploring point of view and narrative structure    21
1.4 Studying screenplays    24
     Extended assignments    29

## Unit Two | Marketing    36

2.1 Creating a brand image    36
2.2 Looking at logos    40
2.3 Marketing a product    44
2.4 Marketing a charity    51
     Extended assignments    54

## Unit Three | Television    58

3.1 Investigating television viewing patterns    58
3.2 Exploring television presentation styles    61
3.3 Exploring television formats    69
3.4 Studying soaps    72
     Extended assignments    75

## Unit Four | Internet    78

4.1 Looking at websites    78
4.2 Designing a personal website    83
4.3 Handling information on a website    86
     Extended assignments    88

## Unit Five | Newspapers | 90

| | | |
|---|---|---|
| 5.1 | Exploring newspaper layout | 90 |
| 5.2 | Examining front page design | 95 |
| 5.3 | Studying photojournalism | 97 |
| 5.4 | Exploring news stories | 101 |
| 5.5 | Exploring fact and opinion in newspapers | 106 |
| | Extended assignments | 108 |

## Unit Six | Comparing media | 110

Radio plays
| | | |
|---|---|---|
| 6.1 | A) Advice on writing a radio play | 111 |
| | B) Extract from a radio play | 112 |

Personal record
| | | |
|---|---|---|
| 6.2 | A) Extract from a reference book: Michael Jackson | 114 |
| | B) Interview with Michael Jackson | 115 |

Radio and television commentaries
| | | |
|---|---|---|
| 6.3 | A) Radio commentary | 116 |
| | B) Television commentary | 117 |

Special feature: The *Titanic*
| | | |
|---|---|---|
| 6.4 | A) Advertisement | 118 |
| | B) Message from the royal family | 118 |
| | C) Online profile of James Cameron, director of *Titanic* | 119 |
| | D) Front page of the *Daily Mirror*, 19 April 1912 | 120 |
| | E) Review of the movie, *Titanic* | 121 |

## Glossary | Media terms | 124

| | |
|---|---|
| *Framework for Teaching English* matching chart | **126** |

# Introduction for students

You already know a huge amount about the media. From your early childhood you will have been bombarded by words and images in advertising, films and television. You will be able to hum jingles from advertisements, remember dialogue from films and cartoons, and spot actors who play different roles in different programmes.

*Developing Media Skills* aims to develop your existing knowledge. Using a range of resources, it will increase your understanding of the decisions involved in different media and explore the way various techniques are used. For example:

- how do directors use moving images to tell their stories without using any dialogue?
- what does the language of a television commercial tell us about its target audience?
- how do newspaper picture editors choose images to match the news stories?

The book is structured into units. These are designed to give you deeper knowledge about different media forms. We have not tried to cover every media form; that would make the book very disjointed. Instead, the aim is to focus on a small number of highly influential media forms – newspapers, film, marketing, television and the Internet. Each unit contains activities and assignments based on objectives from the National Curriculum and the *Framework for Teaching English*.

Most importantly, they contain the kinds of activities that will:

- build your knowledge and understanding
- help you to improve your reading, writing and speaking and listening
- encourage you to think about the effect the media has.

I hope you will enjoy using the book. I would also welcome any direct feedback using the email address below.

*Geoff Barton*

geoff.barton@heinemann.co.uk

## Introduction

Film communicates using moving images and, usually, dialogue. This unit explores the way films are put together. Think about films that have affected you. Which films have made the biggest impact on your life? Do the same films work on video as they do on the big screen? How much do you know about the processes of film-making?

In this unit you will:
• look at images and interpret what they mean
• look at how sequences of images can be used to tell stories and create storyboards to do this
• learn how film can explore different points of view
• explore screenplays and how to write them.

## 1.1 Messages through images

### Objectives

• Look at the way signs and symbols can communicate meanings.
• Compare different interpretations of media texts including images.

As a starting-point for looking at films, think about the way we respond to single images. We use images to communicate ideas all the time. Think of product logos, signs, images in advertising. Think of road signs. It is vital that they communicate information clearly and quickly.

### Activity one

Look at the UK road signs on the next page.
Examine the way they communicate.

Using a table like the one below, examine each sign, saying:
• what its message is
• whether there is any message built into the shape or colour of the sign.

| Sign | Message | How the colour/shape etc... helps to communicate the message |
|------|---------|------------------------------------------------------------|
| A | | |
| B | | |
| C | | |

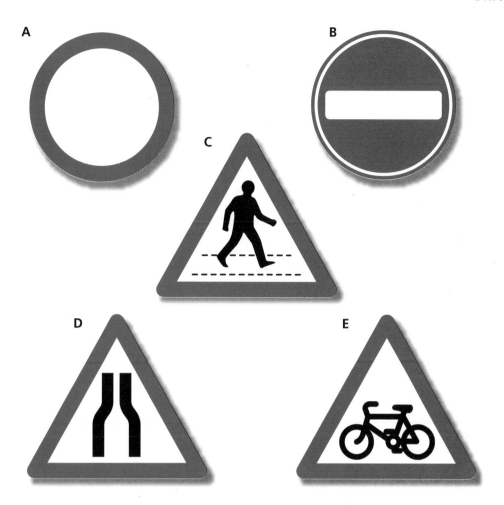

## Activity two

Imagine you have been asked to design some new signs to use around your school. Because they need to make sense to all visitors, whatever their language, you are not allowed to use words.

Work in pairs or small groups to come up with some possibilities. Then present them to the rest of the class. Ask the class to guess what each one means.

You could design signs for the messages below, or come up with your own ideas:
• Welcome
• Dining hall this way
• Fire exit.

 **Web assignment**
Use the table from our website, www.heinemann.co.uk/devmediaskills, to collect examples of signs you see during the journey home from school, or on a visit to the supermarket.

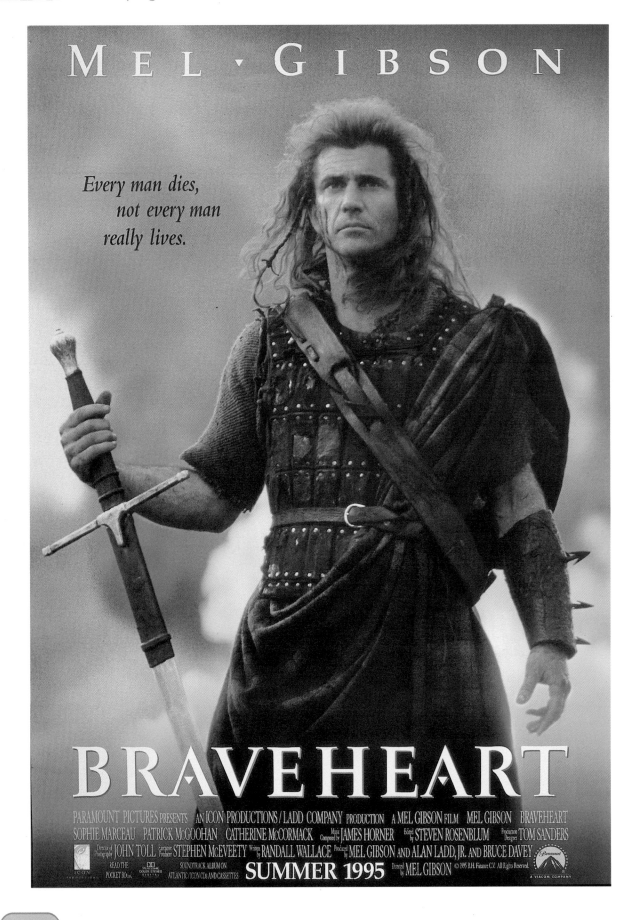

## Activity three

Now look at the way images are used in film posters. They guide us to the type or genre of a film.

### Film elements

- action scenes
- epic scenes
- suspense
- romance
- fantasy
- heroism
- history
- comedy
- spying
- violence
- war
- intrigue
- stunt sequences

| Elements (choose which are relevant from the list) | Which image suggests this and why |
|---|---|
|  |  |
|  |  |
|  |  |
|  |  |
|  |  |

1 The collection of images in the poster opposite suggests some ideas of the different elements of the film. Use the list and a table like the one above to say which elements you think are suggested and which image in the poster tells you this.

2 Look more closely at the figure of Mel Gibson. What does the image suggest about the character he plays? Make a list or draw a spider diagram containing three to five words implied by the image (e.g. proud).

3 Imagine you wanted to change the impression created by the image of Mel Gibson. Imagine he was the villain of the film and you wanted to show negative qualities. How would you change the picture?

## Activity four

Now practise interpreting images using the two classic film posters on pages 12 and 13.

Study the way images are used.

Choose one of the posters.

1 Think of words to explain what elements are suggested by the images (use the list above e.g. romance, intrigue).

2 How would you change the use of images:
- if you wanted to attract a more modern audience?
- if the film was aimed at a younger audience (e.g. 8–12)?

## Assignment

1 Read the brief below from a studio marketing department. They want ideas for promoting a new film. Brainstorm ideas for the way you would use images in a poster.

2 Think about:
- how you will suggest the movie genre (thriller)
- what the central image will be (Guy?)
- whether you will use background images (car crash? city? criminals? his family searching for him?).

3 Then present your ideas to the rest of the group.

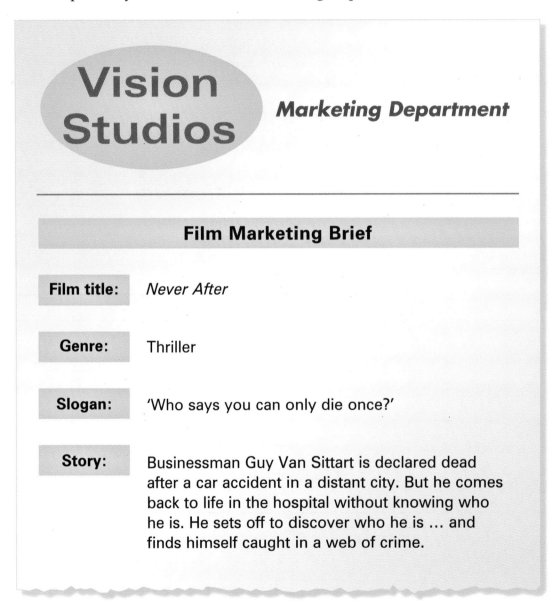

**Vision Studios**  *Marketing Department*

### Film Marketing Brief

**Film title:** *Never After*

**Genre:** Thriller

**Slogan:** 'Who says you can only die once?'

**Story:** Businessman Guy Van Sittart is declared dead after a car accident in a distant city. But he comes back to life in the hospital without knowing who he is. He sets off to discover who he is ... and finds himself caught in a web of crime.

# 1.2 Sequencing images

## Objectives

- Explore how sequences of moving images can tell stories.
- Look at the way meanings change in different media forms.

You will have seen from film posters how single images can inform, persuade and entertain a reader. Now look at the way sequences of images can be used to tell stories. Think, for example, of comics and graphic novels.

Graphic novels are often comics with more adult themes – such as science fiction, fantasy and horror. Like comics, they tell their stories using a sequence of images. But unlike most comics they avoid cartoon styles and use much more vivid, exciting drawing styles.

Look at the two-page extract overleaf from the graphic novel *Aliens: Nightmare Asylum*, by Mark Verheiden and Den Beauvais. You will see that the words have been deleted and replaced by letters.

## Activity 1

1 The pages overleaf contain eight separate story frames. Frames are the separate images used to make up a storyboard or film. Draw a grid like the one below (you will need the third column later). Describe what happens in each frame.

| Frames 1–8 | What happens? | |
|---|---|---|
| 1 | | |
| 2 | | |
| 3 | | |
| 4 | | |
| 5 | | |

2 What dialogue do you think might be taking place in the speech bubbles? Choose three speech bubbles and write down what words you think might be spoken.

| Speech bubble | What might be being said? |
|---|---|
| A | |
| B | |
| C | |

Now look at the way that frames are put together. Graphic novels, like films, use a variety of framing techniques. Look at this glossary to learn more about framing:

| Extreme close up (ECU): | Close up (CU): | Medium Close Up (MCU): |
|---|---|---|
| A shot of the character's eye. | Head and neck. | Head and shoulders. |

| Medium Shot (MS): | Medium Long Shot (MLS): | Long Shot (LS): |
|---|---|---|
| Head to waist. | Head to lower leg. | Full body shot. |

**Extreme Long Shot (ELS):**

The character standing in the distance.

**Point of View (POV):**
A shot where the camera has the same viewpoint as a particular character, showing the audience exactly what that character is seeing.

**Distance of Framing:**
The distance between the camera and the subject being recorded.

## Activity two

Now look again at the grid you created in Activity one, describing what happens in each frame of the graphic novel. In the third column, write down the type of shot there is in each frame: ECU, LS, and so on. Describe what effect this choice of frame has.

Storyboarding is an important process in film-making. Before a film is shot, a storyboard of images is produced. It is easy to forget that all films begin as storyboards. They help the director to visualise what the movie will look like before having an expensive crew and cast on set.

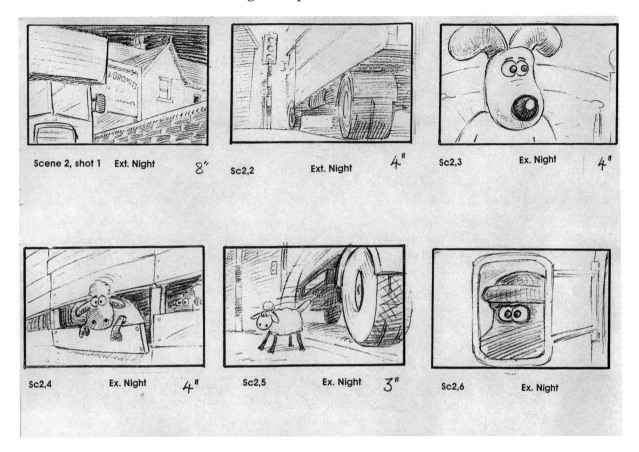

Scene 2, shot 1   Ext. Night   8″

Sc2,2   Ext. Night   4″

Sc2,3   Ex. Night   4″

Sc2,4   Ex. Night   4″

Sc2,5   Ex. Night   3″

Sc2,6   Ex. Night

This storyboard is from the film *A Close Shave*. It shows Shaun the sheep making his escape from the wool-rustlers' lorry. Notice how the graphic artist uses a quick sequence of images to move the story forward. There are also a variety of different shots (a close up of Gromit in the third frame, a long shot of Shaun in the fifth) which help to make the sequence visually interesting.

## Activity three

In class or at home, watch the opening 10–30 seconds of any film. Watch it several times and, using a storyboard frame, sketch out the way the film has been constructed as a sequence of images.

Using the glossary, label each shot to show what type of framing is being used.

 Use the storyboard frame from our website, www.heinemann.co.uk/devmediaskills.

## Assignment

Choose a well-known story (see the suggestions below) and create a 12–16 frame storyboard which tells the story. For each frame, write down the type of shot you want to use, aiming to have a variety of close-ups and long-shots. Write down why you chose each shot and what effect you are trying to create.

Remember that this is not really a test of your drawing skills. It is about how well you can sequence frames to tell a story and choose shots to focus on different elements. If your sketching skills are not good, do the best you can, and place a small caption (label) beneath each frame to explain what happens and what type of shot it is.

Story choices:

- a novel you have read as a class
- a book that you particularly like
- a fairy tale.

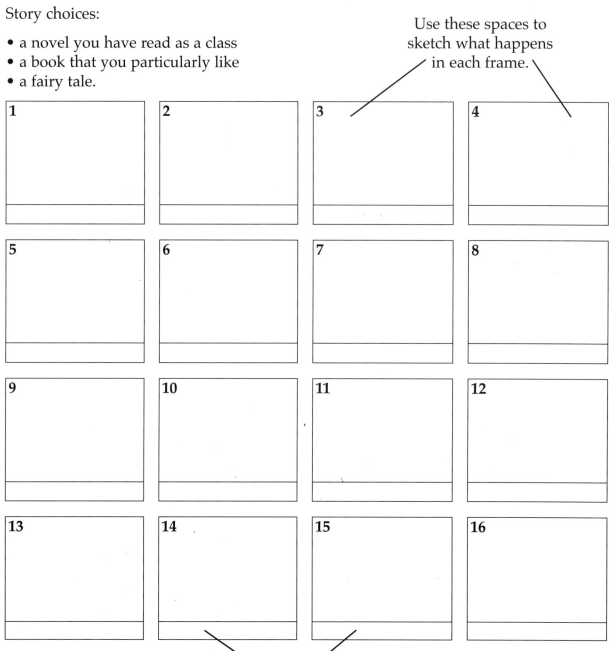

Use these spaces to sketch what happens in each frame.

Use these spaces to label what type of shot you would use for each frame.

# 1.3 Exploring point of view and narrative structure

## Objectives

- Investigate the way stories are structured using storyboarding techniques.
- Explore how point of view can tell stories in different ways.

Storyboarding is a technique used in films, television and advertising to construct a story before filming begins. It allows directors to plan the exact shots they will take.

In films, as in written stories, writers tell the story from different points of view. For example, in a novel the writer might:

- tell the story using an *omniscient* (all-knowing) style. This means that the writer tells us what is going on and what the characters are saying and thinking. For example:
  *The two children walked into the sweet-shop. The owner of the shop looked at them suspiciously. 'I don't like the look of those two,' she thought. The two children looked up at the owner. 'I don't like the look of her,' thought Tom.*

  Notice how the omniscient style can tell us everything we need to know – including what characters are thinking and feeling.

- Use a *first person* style and tell the story from the point of view of a character. For example:
  *As we walked into the shop, I felt the gaze of the owner. She was looking at me over the counter, and she seemed very unhappy with what she saw. I didn't like the look of her much either.*

  This helps us to learn about one character from the inside – seeing what s/he sees. It is also a good technique for building tension, because the writer can hold back information.

- Use either style but mislead the reader – for example, showing us something through the character's eyes … which later turns out to be wrong. Look what happens if the scene in the sweetshop is written like this:
  *As we walked into the sweetshop I noticed the owner. She looked up from the counter towards me. 'What a sweet old lady,' I thought to myself.*

  This allows the writer to build tension because the character has misunderstood what the owner is like. He thinks she seems friendly and kind. Later we will learn that she is in fact very suspicious.

## Activity one

Use the omniscient and first person techniques outlined on page 21 and create the first three frames of a storyboard for each one. Show how the story would begin when told from the two different points of view. Underneath each version, write a comment about the way your storyboard opening works. For example: *to tell the story from the point of view of the customer, my first frame begins outside the shop. It shows the sweetshop door being pushed open ...*

You do not have to draw images in each frame if you do not want to (though real storyboards do have drawings). Instead you can write down exactly what the frame should contain (e.g. *the shopkeeper behind the counter; a close up of her face...* ).

 Use the storyboard layout from our website.

**Example A : omniscient**

| 1 | 2 | 3 |
|---|---|---|
|   |   |   |

**Example B : first-person**

| 1 | 2 | 3 |
|---|---|---|
|   |   |   |

## Cutting between frames

Film makers might also use editing to cut from one storyline to another. This can create different narratives going on at the same time, sometimes called dual or split narratives. Take the story of *Little Red Riding Hood* and look at how it could be structured using different points of view and split narratives:

Frame one: point of view of the wolf. We are looking around a tree at a small cottage in the woods. Long shot.

Cut to: Red Riding Hood putting on her cape. Close up of Little Red Riding Hood looking up at mother as mother says 'and remember – stay on the path'.

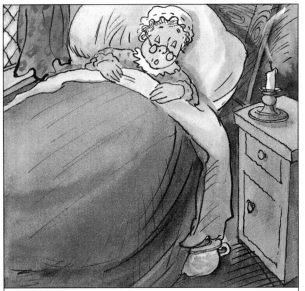

Cut to: Grandma in cottage, in bed, snoring.

Cut to: point of view of the wolf. We do not see him, but we hear his breathing. We are now close to the cottage and about to look in through the window.

Cutting between frames has many effects. Notice:
- how this cutting moves the story forward
- how the different narratives build tension
- how using point of view builds suspense about what the wolf looks like and what he is going to do.

## Assignment

Either continue this narrative sequence, showing what happens next, or use the same device to retell the opening of another story.

For example:
Boy witnesses car being stolen; borrows mobile phone to call police; police arrive; discover person was breaking into his/her own car because the keys are trapped inside.

Think about how you will structure the story. Focus on:
- point of view (e.g. showing us the scene from the eyes of one character).
  Do you tell it from the point of view of:
    – the boy (where is he? what does he see?) *or*
    – the motorist (trying to get into car. Does she notice the boy?) *or*
    – the police (on patrol – receive message; drive fast; arrive on scene. What do they see?)
- narrative structure (e.g. using a dual narrative cutting between storylines)
- type of shot (e.g. close-up, etc).

Use a storyboard with labels (to show point of view, type of shot). Aim to use around 12 frames to show the first part of your story.

# 1.4 Studying Screenplays

## Objectives

- To explore the writing conventions of screenplays and how they differ from other forms of storywriting.
- To analyse the opening of a screenplay.

A screenplay is the written text for a film. It contains dialogue, stage directions and descriptions of characters and setting. Writing a screenplay is a special art. The writer needs to be able to visualise scenes on screen and to remember that you can tell stories through images and actions with no words at all.

Nick Park is one of Britain's most famous animators. Two of his best known creations are Wallace and Gromit who were first featured in the BAFTA-winning film, *A Grand Day Out*. Nick works at Aardman Animations. As well as producing *A Grand Day Out*, Aardman have made lots of successful animated films including *A Close Shave* and *The Wrong Trousers*.

As with all films, before Aardman's productions get to the screen, many people from different departments use their expertise to help create the end product.

The diagram below shows how people from different departments contribute to the making of an animated film.

**Nick Park**

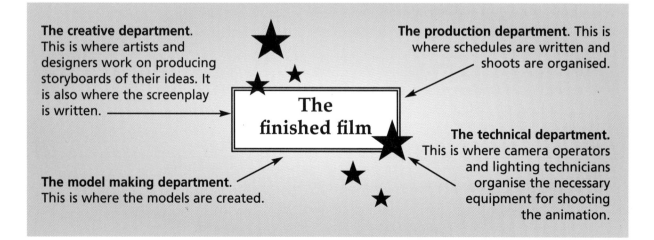

**The creative department.** This is where artists and designers work on producing storyboards of their ideas. It is also where the screenplay is written.

**The production department.** This is where schedules are written and shoots are organised.

**The finished film**

**The model making department.** This is where the models are created.

**The technical department.** This is where camera operators and lighting technicians organise the necessary equipment for shooting the animation.

The diagram at the bottom of page 24 shows some of the key people who are involved in making an animated film. It is vital that the crew create the right atmosphere and achieve the intention of the script in each shot. A screenplay contains the script and the directions for the crew. As such, it is a vital set of instructions for everyone involved.

## Activity one

The extract below is from the Aardman website. It explains how important it is that everything goes smoothly once all the preparation for the film has been completed. Read through the extract.

1 Do you think it is more or less difficult to make an animated film than a film with real actors and actresses? Explain your answer.

2 Why do you think that animators tend to act out the movements of the characters? How would a screenplay help them to do this?

The studios are where the critical process of animation itself takes place. All the work that has gone into the preparation must be orchestrated so that an animator can achieve a strong performance in front of the camera. He or she is backed up by a team of skilled people which is similar to the team on 'live action' shoot.

Often, the director on a shoot is the animator or principal animator. As Director their role is to interpret the storyboard shot by shot in a way that achieves the intention of the script.

The Lighting Cameraperson is extremely important, creating the look and the atmosphere of a scene through the lighting.

Once a setup is in place for a scene, the set is 'hot' and 'crew only' as an accidental bump into a light, model or set can ruin continuity and lose days of work.

Often animators will act out the movements of the characters themselves bringing a certain theatrically to the atmosphere in the studio.

*Aardman Animations*

## Activity two

A Grand Day Out was the first film featuring Wallace and Gromit and was all about them going to the moon. Work in pairs and read through the opening of the screenplay on the next three pages.

• One of you should read the directions.
• The other person should read Wallace.
• Gromit, of course, doesn't speak.

As well as following the story, look at the way the text is written. It shows you the conventions of screenplay writing.

Once you have read through the opening sequence, use the questions which follow to explore in more detail the way the screenplay has been written.

This column lists the action. It details what will be *seen* in the section being filmed.

This instructs the camera to move in and give a close up panoramic shot of the travel magazines and globe.

These lines describe what the character – in this case Wallace – will be doing.

This column lists all the dialogue.

## A Grand Day Out

ACTION

DIALOGUE

Camera pans closely over travel magazines and globe. Wallace and his dog Gromit are at home, browsing through magazines and books.

WALLACE:
Eeeeeh, these bank holidays, it's a problem to decide. Tell you what, Gromit lad! Let's have a nice hot cup of tea, mmm?
Kettle should've boiled by now.

Wallace pours the tea and opens the fridge.

WALLACE:
No cheese Gromit!
Not a bit in the house!

Wallace walks back into the living room with a tray.

WALLACE:
Gromit! That's it! Cheese!
We'll go somewhere where there's cheese!
Now, where are the places you find cheese... Lancashire, Cheddar, Wensleydale, Philadelphia, Tesco's.

They stop and look out of the window at the moon.

WALLACE:
......Everybody knows the moon's made of cheese.

Rats run around the floor as Wallace enters the cellar. He begins to draw out plans to build a rocket, and whistles to Gromit to help. Various stages of building are accompanied by noises, culminating in shots of the finished rocket.

For clarity, the character's name is in capitals with the dialogue immediately underneath.

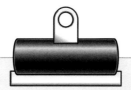

WALLACE:
Everything seems to be under control...
WOAH!

Wallace has a slight accident as
he climbs into the rocket.

WALLACE:
Sixty seconds to blast off.

Gromit operates the machinery
whilst Wallace gives instructions.

WALLACE:
Ooooh. Allotment doors!

The vegetable garden above
the cellar opens up to reveal
the rocket.

WALLACE:
Ooooooh. Emmmmm... No crackers
Gromit! We've forgotten the
crackers!
Whoa... oa... a. Wooaaaa!

Wallace runs out of the rocket
and into the kitchen to get the
crackers. He returns just as the
fuse rope ends. The rocket
takes off watched by an
audience of rats.

WALLACE:
Hold on Gromit. Hold on!

Lots of Oooh and HAhh sounds.
Interior of rocket. Gromit plays
cards as Wallace reads the paper.
Restless, Wallace puts down the
paper and takes a photograph.

WALLACE:
One for the album!

Wallace makes some toast.

WALLACE:
Whu?
Nicely done!

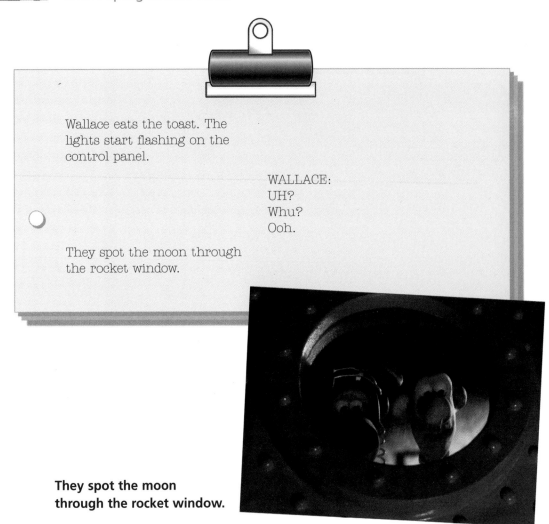

Wallace eats the toast. The lights start flashing on the control panel.

WALLACE:
UH?
Whu?
Ooh.

They spot the moon through the rocket window.

**They spot the moon through the rocket window.**

## Analysing the screenplay

1 Talk about what happens in the opening scene. What is the audience being told about: • where the film is set? • who the characters are? • what will happen?

2 What do we learn about the character of Wallace from the extract? Think of three to five words to describe him.

3 Now look at the way Gromit is portrayed. Although he has no spoken lines, what do we learn about him from: • his actions? • the way Wallace talks to him? • his reactions to Wallace?

4 If this were the opening of a novel, rather than a screenplay, how might it be written? Write a paragraph as if it were the beginning of the novel *A Grand Day Out*.

## Assignment

Based on the screenplay, draw a sketch of what the first six to nine frames of a storyboard might look like for this scene. Think about, what types of shot you would use for each frame, whose point of view you would use and when you would cut from one scene to another.

# Extended assignments

## Speaking and listening

**A** Play 'Desert Island Films'. Everyone in your group should say which one film they would want to take on video with them if cast away on a desert island. They should say:
• what the film is about
• something about the main characters
• what is particularly interesting or enjoyable about the film.

Now, based on the work you have done in this section, include some comments about the way the film is constructed. You might look at the opening or some other sequence. Comment on:
• the way the story is told
• how the director moves from one shot to another
• what we learn about characters from a) their words and
  b) their actions.

Ideally, try to play a short video clip of a key moment and then comment on what it shows about the film – for example, the dialogue, the characterisation, the use of music or special effects, the style of camera work or editing. Try to make a comment about how the film is made, as well as what it is about.

**B** Hold a media debate.
Read the opinion below:

'The idea of film classification is silly. To call some films PG or 15 or 18 doesn't work. Some people at the age of 15 are mature enough to see an 18-rated film. Other people aged 25 probably aren't mature enough. Film classification should be scrapped.'

• What are the arguments for and against classification of films?
• Should there be different rules for videos?

Hold a debate within a small group or your whole class, with some people putting the case **for** and others putting the case **against** film censorship.

 There are further guidelines for running a formal debate on our website, www.heinemann.co.uk/devmediaskills.

## Romeo and Juliet

Since the early days of movie-making around the beginning of the twentieth century, there have been many film versions of Shakespeare's *Romeo and Juliet*. Some of these are adaptations of the play; some of them use the play as a loose version of a modern love story; some are ballet and dance versions; some are foreign versions of the film.

1 As a class, discuss why you think so many people have wanted to make a film version of Romeo and Juliet.

2 Now look at the posters below. As you do so, think about the following questions. You should share your ideas with a partner.

- What can you tell from the posters about what the films will be like?
- What central image does each of the posters use?
- Why do you think the film-makers have chosen this image for the poster?

**Poster from Franco Zeffirelli's adaptation, (1968).**

**Poster from Renato Castellani's adaptation, (1954).**

**Poster from Baz Luhrman's adaptation, (1996).**

## From playscript to screenplay

When you write a story or poem, you are usually writing directly for your reader. A screenplay is different. It is more like a set of instructions for other people including actors, directors and the technical crew.

The screenplay aims to tell the story, but also to show how that story should be presented on screen. It will contain words to be spoken by the actors, but also directions that create a picture of how the scene should look.

## Reading

On the next two pages is an extract from Shakespeare's *Romeo and Juliet*, together with a film adaptation of the same scene. The scene is taken from the end of the play (Act V, Scene III), where Romeo comes into the tomb and finds Juliet apparently dead. He kills himself.

**a** In what ways is the screenplay different from the original version?
**b** How does the writer paint a picture of the scene for the director and actors?
**c** How does the writer use film techniques to tell the story?
**d** How does the writer add drama to the scene?

## Writing

**a** What advice would you give to the actor playing the part of Romeo? How should he play the part?

Use the writing frame below to give some ideas on how he should approach the part.

> Here is my advice about how you should move during the scene...
>
> The camera will sometimes focus in close up on your face. Here's the way you should look...

**b** Using the table like the one below, choose three different lines or quotations from the original screenplay and give advice to the actor playing Romeo on how he should speak them.

| Choose three different lines or quotations here. | Give advice to the actor playing Romeo on how to speak them here. |
|---|---|
| 1 | |
| 2 | |
| 3 | |

## A: Extract from *Romeo and Juliet*. Act V Scene III

**Romeo:** O my love, my wife!
Death that hath sucked the honey of thy breath
Hath had no power yet upon thy beauty.
Thou art not conquered; beauty's **ensign** yet
Is crimson in thy lips and in thy cheeks,
And death's pale flag is not advanced there.
Tybalt, liest thou there in thy bloody sheet?
O what more favour can I do to thee,
Than with that hand that cut thy youth in twain
To sunder his that was thine enemy?
Forgive me cousin. Ah dear Juliet,
Why art thou yet so fair? Shall I believe
That **unsubstantial death is amorous**,
And that the lean **abhorred** monster keeps
Thee here in dark to be his **paramour?**
For fear of that, I still will stay with thee,
And never from this palace of dim night
Depart again. Here, here will I remain
With worms that are my chamber-maids. O here
Will I set up my everlasting rest;
And **shake the yoke of inauspicious stars**
From this world-wearied flesh. Eyes look your last.
Arms, take your last embrace. And lips, O you
The doors of breath, **seal with a righteous kiss**
A **dateless bargain to engrossing death**.
*[Takes out the poison]* **Come bitter conduct, come unsavoury guide.**
**Thou desperate pilot, now at once run on**
**The dashing rocks thy sea-sick weary bark.**
Here's to my love! *[drinks]* O true apothecary!
Thy drugs are quick. Thus with a kiss I die.

   *Enter* FRIAR LAWRENCE, *with lantern, crow and spade*

**by a dead man interred:** literally, buried by a dead man. Romeo is going to kill himself and sees
  himself as already dead.

**lightning:** lightening

**ensign:** flag carried in battle. Romeo is talking about the battle between life and death for
  possession of Juliet's body.

**unsubstantial death is amorous:** bodiless death is in love (with Juliet)

**abhorred:** that we shrink from in horror

**paramour:** lover

**shake the ... stars:** shake off the burden imposed by fate

**seal with ... death:** make an eternal bargain with death that wants to take possession of our lives
  and seal with a kiss

**Come bitter ... bark:** Romeo compares his willpower to the pilot and his body to the boat which
  is being steered onto the rocks of death.

## B: Screenplay adaptation of *Romeo and Juliet*

**INT.** CHURCH. NIGHT
Romeo walks down the aisle. **CU** of his strained face.
**CUT TO:** altar, with dim shape of body before it. **POV** Romeo, camera unstable as if we are looking through his eyes as he walks.

**CUT TO: CU** of Juliet's pale face through the cloth.
**CUT TO: CU** of Romeo's face, the stress almost tearing it apart. He looks up as if to ask 'why?' then back down at his love.

> ROMEO
> O my love, my wife!
> Death that hath sucked the honey of thy breath
> Hath had no power yet upon thy beauty.

Romeo is drawing the veil from Juliet's face.
**CUT TO:** Romeo's face, this time tears clearly swelling in his eyes as he looks down. He can hardly speak.

> ROMEO
> Thou art not conquered; beauty's ensign yet
> Is crimson in thy lips and in thy cheeks,
> And death's pale flag is not advanced there.

CU on Romeo as he stares intently at Juliet. Her features are so perfect that she could almost be asleep.

> ROMEO
> Ah, dear Juliet,
> Why art thou yet so fair?

**CUT TO: LS** showing him holding Juliet in his arms. A bird flutters high overhead, making him look up. A beam of light slices through the darkness. Romeo looks again at Juliet.
**CUT TO:** her face.
**CUT TO:** his face, tears on his cheeks now.

> ROMEO
> Shall I believe
> That unsubstantial death is amorous,
> And that the lean abhorred monster keeps
> Thee here in dark to be his paramour?

Romeo gently kisses Juliet.
Romeo reaches for the vial and, slowly, opens it. Looking intently at Juliet, he drinks it.

> ROMEO
> Eyes look your last.
> Arms, take your last embrace. And, lips, O you
> The doors of breath, seal with a righteous kiss
> A dateless bargain to engrossing death.

He finishes the vial and winces slightly. Her hand tightens on his.
**CUT TO:** his eyes intently staring at hers.
The vial falls to the floor and smashes. Another bird flaps overhead, disturbed by the sound.
**CUT TO:** her eyes open.
**CUT TO:** his eyes, suddenly seeming to realise that she is not dead. His face contorts.
**CUT TO:** her face.
**CUT TO:** Romeo crumbles to the church floor.

> JULIET
> (Mouths the word but cannot speak it) Romeo.

**INT:** Interior. Directors need to know whether they have to film indoors or outdoors.
**CU:** Close up.
**POV:** Point of view (in this case, the point of view of Romeo).
**CUT TO:** Move the camera to.
**LS:** Long shot.

## Writing

This is the opening of a poem written by Alfred Noyes at the start of the twentieth century. It tells the tale of a highwayman who arranges to meet his lover Bess – only to be thwarted by Tom who has overheard their plans.

### *The Highwayman*
by Alfred Noyes

**Part One**

**I**

The wind was a **torrent** of darkness among the gusty trees,
The moon was a ghostly galleon tossed upon cloudy seas,
The road was a ribbon of moonlight, over the purple moor,
And the highwayman came riding-
      Riding-riding-
The highwayman came riding, up to the old inn-door.

**II**

He'd a **French cocked-hat** on his forehead, a bunch of lace at his chin,
A coat of the claret velvet, and breeches of brown **doe-skin**;
They fitted with never a wrinkle: his boots were up to the thigh!
And he rode with a jewelled twinkle,
      His **pistol butts** a-twinkle,
His **rapier hilt a-twinkle**, under the jewelled sky.

**III**

Over the cobbles he clattered and clashed in the dark inn-yard,
And he tapped with his whip on the shutters, but all was locked and barred;
He whistled a tune to the window, and who should be waiting there
But the landlord's black-eyed daughter,
      Bess, the landlord's daughter,
Plaiting a dark red love-knot into her long black hair.

**IV**

And dark in the old inn-yard a stable-wicket creaked
Where Tim the **ostler** listened; his face was white and peaked;
His eyes were hollows of madness, his hair like mouldy hay,
But he loved the landlord's daughter,
      The landlord's red-lipped daughter,
Dumb as a dog he listened, and he heard the robber say-

## V

'One kiss, my bonny sweetheart, I'm after a prize to-night,
But I shall be back with the yellow gold before the morning light;
Yet, if they press me sharply, and **harry me** through the day,
Then look for me by moonlight,
      Watch for me by moonlight,
I'll come to thee by moonlight, though hell should bar the way.'

## VI

He rose upright in the stirrups; he scarce could reach her hand,
But she loosened her hair i' the **casement!** His face burnt like a brand
As the black cascade of perfume came tumbling over his breast;
And he kissed its waves in the moonlight,
      (Oh, sweet black waves in the moonlight!)
Then he tugged at his rein in the moonlight, and galloped away to the West.

---

**Glossary**

**Torrent**: fast-moving stream or river

**French cocked-hat:** pointed hat worn in the 17th and 18th century (for example, worn by Napoleon Bonaparte)

**Doe-skin:** skin of a female deer

**Pistol butts:** handle of his gun

**Rapier hilt a-twinkle:** the handle of his sword sparkles

**Ostler:** someone who looks after horses

**Harry me:** pressure me

**Casement:** window

---

The poem is famous for its dramatic storyline and powerful rhythms. It is also highly visual, with lots of reference to colours and moody atmosphere – making it ideal for a film.

Imagine you have been commissioned to make a film of *The Highwayman*.

1  Plan a storyboard, showing what the opening sequence of, say, eight to twelve frames would show. Remember to consider point of view and different ways of structuring the story. You may, for example, wish to change the order of the story around.

Think about:
- what your opening shot will be
- where you will start the story
- how you will show the setting
- what types of camera shots will work best for different shots.

2  Write the opening sequence of a film screenplay based on the poem and storyboard. Think about the characters you will need. Indicate whether each scene is interior (int) or exterior (ext).

Look back at the screenplays of *A Grand Day Out* and *Romeo and Juliet* to remind yourself of the writing conventions.

# Marketing

## Introduction

This unit is about more than advertising. Marketing means thinking about how best to sell or promote a product. The product could be anything from cat food to a political party to a new band.

In this unit you will:
- learn how product names are developed and look at the impact words can have on an audience
- learn how logos are used to create memorable brands
- explore how a marketing campaign is developed
- look at how marketing can promote charities as well as companies and products.

## 2.1 Creating a brand image

### Objectives

- Explore ways in which product names are developed.
- Look at the history and associations of some product names.

Marketing is made up of several different processes. When people talk about marketing they may be referring to one or all of the following processes:

- researching the market – what people buy, want, or think about particular products or issues
- identifying gaps in the market for new products
- thinking up a product name
- creating a brand image (e.g. a logo, a jingle, a slogan) so that customers feel that the product has a clear identity
- devising an advertising campaign in one or more media (e.g. television and radio commercials, newspaper advertisements)
- launching the product (e.g. arranging for an author to sign copies of a new book on the day it arrives in the shops).

In this section we will look closely at creating a brand name. Getting the right name for a product is vital.

The car maker Henry Ford launched a car named after his son. It was called the Edsel. The fact that the model flopped is seen by many as a problem with the name rather than the car.

## Activity one

Outlined below are some ways in which product names work. For each category, see if you can think of another example:

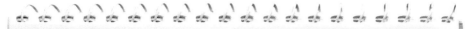

- Kwik Save (playing around with spelling to create a memorable name)
- Coca-cola (alliteration: repetition of initial consonants)
- Brewmaster (personification: an object presented like a person)
- Jaguar (metaphor: the car identified with the grace and power of an animal)
- Magi-Stik (hyperbole: exaggerating a product's effects)
- 7-Up (using a combination of numbers and letters).

## Activity two

Here is a list of product names. The origins of the name have been jumbled up. See if you can match the product to the origin.

| | Name | Product type | Where the name came from (origin) |
|---|---|---|---|
| 1 | Adidas | Sportswear | **a** Danish 'leg godt' – play well |
| 2 | Biro | Pens | **b** Persian god of light |
| 3 | Bovril | Hot drink | **c** Founded by Adolph Dassler, known to friends as Adi. He added the first three letters of his surname to create the product name |
| 4 | Castrol | Oil | **d** German, from the first part of the word fantasy |
| 5 | Fanta | Soft drink | **e** Latin 'hominis vis' – strength of man |
| 6 | Hovis | Bread | **f** Originally made from castor oil |
| 7 | Lego | Toy | **g** Latin 'bovis' – ox. Latin 'virilis' – manly, powerful |
| 8 | Mazda | Light bulbs/cars | **h** Invented by Lazlo Biro |

Which products/origins were easiest to match, and which were most difficult? Why?

## Activity three

In pairs or small groups, devise names for the products below.

Start by thinking about the audience and purpose:
- who is this product for?
- what is it designed to do?

Choose a name that you think works best. Spend time brainstoming different possibilities. Perhaps use a dictionary or thesaurus to help.

Then write a few sentences explaining your chosen name. Set it out like this:

---

Product:

Target audience:

Chosen name:

Rationale:

---

*Rationale = explain why you chose the name. What word does the product name remind you of? What associations has it got (e.g. strength, light, success)?*

**A: New small car model**
*Aimed at carefree rather than serious drivers*

**B: New hairdressing shop**
*Upmarket, sophisticated clients*

**C: New computer**
*Powerful, sleek, aimed at business professionals*

**D: New toothpaste**
*Keeps teeth whiter, breath fresher, using organic ingredients*

**E: New boy band**
*Five members, pure pop/dance tracks, aimed at young teen audience*

## Activity four

As a class, compare the different product names you have devised. Which ones do you think are most successful? Think about why this is. Do short names usually work better than longer ones? Are there any other ingredients that seem to make better product names?

### Assignment

Explore five product names of items you have at home. Look through your fridge or store cupboard for names of food products. Look at the names of cars or computers.

Spend some time researching what the names suggest. Research the word origins (etymology) in a dictionary.

Use a grid like this one to record your research findings. The first one has been done for you.

| Product | Name | Associations | Etymology |
|---------|------|--------------|-----------|
| **1** Breakfast cereal. | Rice Krispies. | Rice = light, healthy Krispies = crunchy, easy to eat, fun (spelt with K rather than C – makes it seem light hearted). | Crisp = old English for wrinkled, rippled Latin = crispus for curled. |
| **2** | | | |
| **3** | | | |
| **4** | | | |
| **5** | | | |

 This assignment is also on our website, www.heinemann.co.uk/devmediaskills. The site also contains links to etymological dictionaries online.

# 2.2 Looking at logos

## Objectives

- Explore visual techniques such as font style in the design of product logos.
- Experiment with different ways of presenting a product name in different visual styles.

One aim of marketing is to make us remember a product. Names of products are therefore often presented in eye-catching, memorable ways. There are so many different products available for people to buy that the marketing of them is an essential way of making sure they are noticed.

## Activity one

Webpromotion is a US company that designs company logos. They believe that simple use of lettering is often the most powerful and successful way of creating an image. They say:

> In our logo design process, we strive to create memorable marks which are clean and professional. When you think of some of the biggest companies, their logos are uncomplicated and professional.

Start by looking at some of their logo designs.

1 Which logo is the simplest? Which is most eye-catching? Give reasons for your answer.

2 Which do you think works the best? Again, say why.

3 Focus on one logo and choose an adjective which best sums up the image it creates from the following list or choose one of your own: professional, traditional, reliable, forward-thinking, modern, advanced, technical, trustworthy, memorable, simple, bold.

## Activity two

1 This page contains four well-known logos. Study them carefully. In pairs, choose one that you and a partner know well.

**2** Now focus on *two* of the product logos that you managed to identify. Discuss what image of the product the logo creates. For this you might use adjectives such as bright, fashionable, fun, lively, surprising, young, exciting, enjoyable, fresh, tasty.

Be as precise as you can in saying *how* each logo creates this impression – e.g. use of colour, size and shape of letters.

**3** Now see if you can draw the logo you and your partner knew well from memory.

Find out:
- how well you knew the logo
- which parts of it (colour, shape, lettering) have stuck in your mind the most?

 **Web assignment**
Research logos using the fact sheet on our website, www.heinemann.co.uk/devmediaskills. Identify product logos you like and analyse how they work.

## Assignment

The Webpromotion logos use simple font and design styles to create memorable brands. Divide into groups and using a word-processor or desktop publisher, try to do the same. Use this memo to get you started.

---

### Memo

| | |
|---|---|
| **From:** | B Stones, Chief Executive |
| **To:** | Marketing team |
| **Re:** | Logo Design |

Some of our major clients have requested new logos for their products. Please use the following product briefs and come up with a number of possible designs for us. We would then like you to make a presentation, showing us which designs you recommend and why.

Above all, we want the logos to be:
**1 simple**
**2 eye-catching**
**3 easy to remember.**

*Remember – we only want logos, not slogans or storyboards.*

---

## Products:

**Sleepwell**

| | |
|---|---|
| *Product:* | traditional beds |
| *Target buyer:* | middle aged |
| *Image:* | comfortable, relaxing beds that will help you get a good night's sleep |

**Pzazz!**

| | |
|---|---|
| *Product:* | new chocolate bar. Inside the chocolate is a surprising sherbet taste. |
| *Target buyer:* | young (9–16) |
| *Image:* | fun, exciting, surprising snack |

**Timestyle**

| | |
|---|---|
| *Product:* | watches for people who want their watches to be noticed |
| *Target buyer:* | 16–30 |
| *Image:* | colourful but sophisticated watches |

## Evaluation

Each group should then present its finished logos to the other groups.
Explain your approach.

- What were you trying to achieve in your design?
- How does the design communicate the image of the product?
- What decision-making process did you go through?
- How did you decide what features to leave in and which to leave out?

How successful do you think the logos were?

# 2.3 Marketing a product

**Objectives**

- Explore the way a marketing campaign is developed.
- Compare the presentation of ideas in different text types.

UK consumers enjoy eating chocolate and sweets. That is why our shops contain such a large range of products. This means marketing teams have to work hard to get their product noticed. Giving it the right image aimed at the right target audience is vital.

Explore the way M&M's marketing team developed a recent campaign.

# M&M's marketing campaign

### Stage 1  The product

To appeal to a young audience, the product is given a human personality. For example, one M&M's character is called Red. Here are some of his personality features:

- leader
- mischievous
- smart
- can be catty when provoked.

The team developed a clear view of what Red should look like and produced an artist's guide to make sure that the character is always presented in the same way.

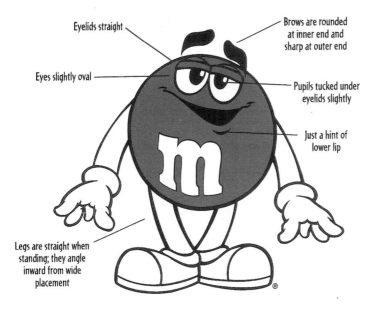

Eyelids straight

Brows are rounded at inner end and sharp at outer end

Eyes slightly oval

Pupils tucked under eyelids slightly

Just a hint of lower lip

Legs are straight when standing; they angle inward from wide placement

## Activity one

1 Why do you think that giving a product a personality will help it to appeal to the target audience?

2 What other products can you think of that have a personality in this way?

3 What kind of products do you think this approach would **not** work for?

### Stage 2 Getting the product known

The marketing team devised the idea of postcards for the different M&M characters. They would be a fun thing for the target audience to see and collect, and would help to communicate the different personalities of the characters.

Look at these three postcards. Notice the wording on each of the cards.

## Activity two

1 The postcards do not mention the product M&M's directly at all.
   How would the target audience recognise the M&M product?

2 How do the designs emphasise the different personalities? Look at the
   way the characters stand, their expression, what they are wearing and
   their colours.

### Stage 3 Storyboard to commercial

As in the making of full-length feature films, TV commercials
start with a storyboard and script.

## Activity three

Read the script opposite carefully. Then sketch out a 9-frame storyboard
showing what the script might look like when filmed. See pages 18–19 for
notes on storyboarding. Do not spend long trying to get the images
looking good. Instead, concentrate on:

• how you would tell the story
• the kinds of shots you would use (e.g. close up, whose point-of-view,
  and so on. To remind yourself of these techniques, see page 18).

 Use the storyboarding frame from the website,
www.heinemann.co.uk/devmediaskills.

## Activity four

Now look at the storyboard used for the actual commercial on page 48 and
compare it with your version.

1 How is the actual storyboard different from yours?

2 What different shots does the director use?

3 How does the director make sure that the M&M's product is kept
   clearly visible?

| Ways that the storyboards are similar | Ways that they are different |
|---|---|
|  |  |
|  |  |

4 Create a grid comparing the actual storyboard to your version, like this:

5 Write a paragraph comparing your storyboard and the actual one.
   Highlight the strengths and weaknesses of each.

Everything in the column labelled 'PICTURE' refers to what will be *seen* throughout the commercial

The column labelled 'SOUND' refers to everything that will be *heard* – e.g. it contains all the dialogue and explains that there will be music throughout.

**BBDO**
**TV**

**Client BBDO Mars Group**          **Date 16.11.99     FINAL SCRIPT**
**Title 'Run'**                              **Timelength 30"**

| **PICTURE** | **SOUND** |
|---|---|
| Open on Red and Yellow on a sofa, lazily watching TV. | **SFX:** Music throughout. |
| A trendy woman rushes in, obviously on her way out. She is dressed in puffer jacket and has sunglasses on. She reaches down to pick up her car keys, and is suddenly startled when she sees the M&M's. | Woman: Who are you two? |
|  | Red M&M's: Just a couple of good looking M&M's sit down. |
| She looks a bit stunned still, pushes the sunglasses on to her head and slowly sits down to perch on the side of the chair. In her hand is a bag of M&M's. | Woman: (Doubtful but quite bossy) The same M&M's that come in a bag? |
| Holds up the bag and looks inside as if for confirmation. | Yellow: The same ones! |
| Red stands up on the sofa. | Red: Only bigger! |
| Woman holds up an M&M in her fingers. | Woman: With a colourful shell … just like this? |
| Red nudges Yellow. | Red: Hey! The babe is catching on! |
|  | Woman: (Keeping her cool) And delicious, milk chocolate inside? |
| Red hits himself over the head. | Red: Yeah! |
| Woman suddenly relaxes back into her chair. | Woman: (All smiles now) Well, isn't that great you guys dropped in … |
|  | Yellow: (suspicious) Why's that? |
| Woman scrunches up her empty bag, and points towards Red and Yellow. | Woman: Because, my little friend, I've just run out …. which one of you is peanut? |
| Red stands up on the sofa and whispers to the camera. | Red: Eh, he is! … I hear he is delicious! So long, buddy! |
| End on Yellow looking nervous. | Yellow: Gulp! |

**SFX** Sound effects

W. Who are you two?
(Long shot)

R. Just a couple of good looking
M&M's

W. The same M&M's that come
in a bag?

Y. The same ones
R. Only bigger!

W. With a colourful shell … just
like this?

R. Hey, the babe is catching on!
W. And delicious milk chocolate
inside?
R. Yeah!

W. Well, isn't that great you
guys dropped in …
Y. Why's that?
(Close up)

W. Because, my little friend I've
just run out … Which one of
you is peanut?
R. Eh, he is! … I hear he is
delicious! So long buddy!

Y. Gulp!

## Activity five

1 In pairs, discuss who you would choose to appear in the commercial. You might comment on:
   - programmes and products s/he is identified with
   - what image s/he might help to create for M&M's
   - which audience s/he is likely to appeal to.

2 How does the language of the different M&M characters show their different personalities. Can you find ways in which they speak differently?

3 How well do you think the commercial works in appealing to its target audience?

## Assignment

Imagine you have been asked to develop an idea for a new M&M – Purple. Working in a small group, or pairs, develop the character's personality from first concept to finished script. The three following stages below will take you through the steps in the process.

**Stage 1**
Devise a personality – what is s/he like?
Brainstorm ideas – key words – personality features.
Here are some possibilities to start you off:

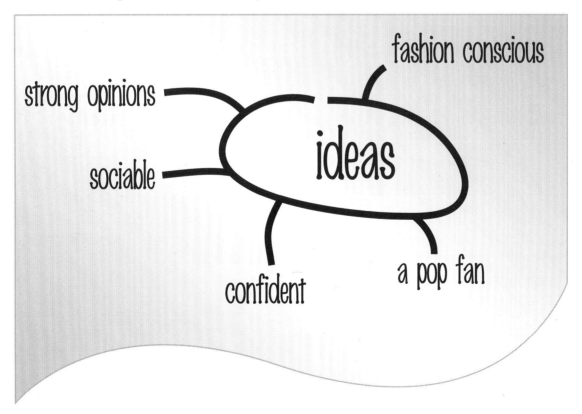

strong opinions

fashion conscious

sociable

ideas

confident

a pop fan

## Stage 2

Develop a sketch of what s/he looks like.
- Think about the shape of the character.
- Look at the way the other M&M's are presented.
- Look at the positioning of eyes and mouth.
- Experiment with different versions of Purple before you complete a final version.

## Stage 3

Plan a story sequence to introduce Purple as a new character. Remember that your main aim is to sell the M&M brand, so the message of the story needs to be clear.

Brainstorm ideas – for example:
- How is Purple introduced?
- How do the other characters react?
- Which human being might also be involved? Think of who you would want to play this part.

Construct a storyboard to show the sequence.

# 2.4 Marketing a charity

## Objectives

- Explore how meaning is communicated in a variety of media texts.
- Practise using persuasive and rhetorical devices.

Most people think that marketing is only about products that we buy – such as the M&M's example. Advertising and marketing is also used to shape our opinions.

## Activity one

Here Derek Warren of the Barnardo's charity describes the marketing approach of one of their 'giving children back their future' campaigns. Basing your answers on his account, identify the aims, audience and main message of the Barnardo's campaign.

### Barnardo's Communications Campaign

We launched the Barnardo's campaign in October 1999 with the clear objective of updating the charity's image. We wanted to increase public understanding of our work and make the organisation more deserving in the eyes of a new generation of potential donors.

Research showed that lots of people recognised the Barnardo's name, but had very low understanding of what it does. The vast majority of people still associate the charity with running 'orphanages'. In fact, this hasn't really been part of our work for the past 25 years.

While the overall awareness message of the campaign was aimed at a general audience, its key target audience was ABC1 adults in the 30–55 age range, with children. So the advertising element of the campaign was restricted to broadsheet and 'middlebrow' tabloid newspapers as the most cost-effective channel for reaching this audience.

The design concept for the advertisements was a scenario to challenge the traditional view of Barnardo's work. Each of the treatments showed a child as if an adult situation. The message was that early action with vulnerable, disadvantaged or abused children and their families can prevent such negative adult outcomes as alcohol or drug dependence, suicide, homelessness, prostitution or imprisonment.

Barnardo's range of work is very varied and difficult to summarise in an easily understandable way. The charity runs over three hundred projects throughout the UK, each of them different. The common factor is the aim of improving the life chances of vulnerable and damaged children and young people.

This approach is encapsulated in the campaign slogan *'Giving children back their future'*.

Derek Warren

## Activity two

Having identified the main message of the Barnardo's campaign, look at the way that it was translated into the newspaper advertisements above.

1 Look back at the target audience, aim and message. How do the advertisements use these?

2 Which advertisement do you find most effective, and why?

3 Some people have been shocked by the advertisements. Why do you think this is?

4 Are there any parts of the advertising campaign that you might have approached differently?

## Assignment

A new local charity has asked you to develop a marketing campaign. Work in a small group and prepare a report or presentation to the charity giving them your advice. Here is their brief to you:

# Neighbourhood citizen scheme

We are a small charity aimed at encouraging people to look after their neighbours – especially where they are old or vulnerable.

We want to promote good citizenship – e.g. dropping in to see that neighbours are well, warm enough, not worried about anything serious.

We require a marketing campaign that gets our message across to people.

Here is the help we need from you:

1 Do we need to change our name? If so, to what?

2 Do we need a slogan or logo? If so, ideas please.

3 How should we promote ourselves – through advertisements, posters, leaflets?

Bear in mind that our budget is small.

We look forward to hearing from you.

Put together your package of advice. Work in pairs or a small group. Think about the unique selling point of the charity and its target audience. Talk about the issues they raise and how best to advise them.

Present your solutions as an A4 report or 2-minute presentation.

# Extended assignments

## Speaking and listening

Some people worry about the way products are marketed at children. Do you think television advertising aimed at young children exploits them? Think about the commercials for toys and sweets on Saturday morning television and, especially, in the run-up to Christmas.

Should such advertising be banned, or controlled more? If so, how? Start by making a list of the arguments for and against.

**(W) Web assignment**

Do a research project on the marketing of products aimed at children – see our website, www.heinemann.co.uk/devmediaskills.

## Reading

The article from *The Guardian* newspaper (opposite) shows how music can be an important part of marketing. In the past a band would record a song; if they were lucky it would be played on the radio; if they were very lucky it became a hit.

The article shows how radio is only part of the marketing of a band. The writer uses a mixture of facts and opinions to make his points. As you read, look out for examples of both.

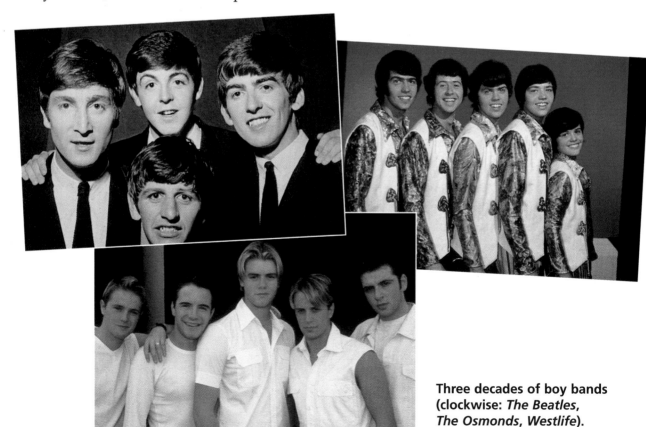

**Three decades of boy bands (clockwise: *The Beatles*, *The Osmonds*, *Westlife*).**

Friday 5 May 2000

# Plug and play

**Dave Simpson**

*Licensing pop songs to TV and commercials is bigger business than ever. Dave Simpson investigates:*

Once upon a time, a good song, radio play and a television live appearance would be enough to guarantee a hit record. Nowadays, with more records being released and more competition than ever before, the music industry is moving into areas of '**subliminal** marketing' to shift its products.

Consider Moby's Play album. In the last few months, the album's killer tracks have featured on countless television adverts and in television programme trailers. 'The Sky is Broken', for example, advertises Galaxy; 'Everloving' plugs Thorntons; 'Bodyrock' sells, inevitably, 'Rolling Rock'. Play even advertises rival products: 'Run On' – now also a hit single – features in a Renault Kangoo advert, while 'Find My Baby' memorably draws admirers towards the Nissan Almera.

There are numerous other tie-ins. Tracks from Play feature in no less than six movie soundtracks (including *The Next Best Thing* and *The Beach*, which uses 'Porcelain', soon to be another hit single) and simply acres of TV exposure. There's 'Match of the Day' (Bodyrock), Sky football (numerous tracks), and Posh Spice's docu-soap, 'Victoria's Secrets' (that's 'Run On' again). In fact, there are so many tie-ins that Moby's record label Mute has virtually lost track of them. 'There may have been something with Adidas as well,' they say. All this before we even get out of England.

In Europe, Moby advertises the Volkswagen Polo ('Porcelain'), Maxwell House coffee ('Run On'), Bosch and France Telecom (both 'Porcelain' again), the Renault Scenic ('Run On') and several more within individual countries including, bizarrely, Bailey's Irish Cream, in Spain. Then there's America... Result? A year after release – it performed only moderately initially – Moby's Play album has sold over a million worldwide and spent the last three weeks as the British number one. ...

'Moby is very hot property at the moment,' confesses John McGrath, head of Mute Publishing, who handle the dome-headed danceman. 'The Nissan Almera ad has done wonders for him. Suddenly everyone else wants to use the music and the album has developed a whole new lease of life. I can't turn on the TV without hearing Moby. I just go ker-ching, it's Moby yet again.' ...

There's nothing new about advertisements selling pop music. The practice boomed in the mid-80s. What has changed markedly, however, is the level of sophistication now involved. 'The song title itself is very important,' reveals McGuinness. 'A couple of years ago there was an ad using an old M People track, "Search for the Hero". Interestingly, the record company didn't re-release it as a single, they just promoted a "best-of" album on the back of the inclusion in the ad. That's an incredibly smart move.'

Sometimes, it's hard to decide whether the record is selling the product, or the product/advert is selling the record.

**Subliminal:** communicating a message that people don't really notice

## Comprehension

**1** The article outlines lots of examples of the way Moby's music is used. Use a grid like the one below to note the main point made in each paragraph.

| Paragraph | Main point |
|-----------|-----------|
| 1 | |
| 2 | |
| 3 | |
| 4 | |
| 5 | |
| 6 | |
| 7 | |

**2** What is the main overall point of the article?

**3 a** The article contains a mixture of facts and opinions. Write down one sentence which is a fact.
   **b** Write down one sentence which is an opinion.

**4** In your own words, say what the writer's opinion is.

**5** In paragraph 2, the writer refers to Moby's 'killer' tracks. What do you think 'killer' means in this context? Write down a different word he might have used instead.

**6** Extended response
Look again at the last sentence of the article. What do you think the writer means by this? Imagine the sentence is the first in a paragraph. Write the rest of the paragraph explaining why it is hard to decide whether the record is selling the product or the product is selling the record.

## Writing

Imagine you work for a major marketing company.

A record company is putting together a new boy band aimed at selling records to the 9–14 market. The members of the band are below. Decide how you would market the band using the prompts below, and write a media proposal.

The band:

**Ben, Jake, Wes, Shane**

1 Brainstorm a name for the band. Look back at page 37 to study the way some product names are devised.

2 Design a logo for the band. See page 40 to remind yourself of the features of different logos.

3 Design a magazine advertisement for a teenage magazine.
   In it you should:
   • introduce the band
   • highlight their new single ('So cold without you').

4 Write your media proposal on one side of A4 saying how you aim to promote the band, the image you would give them, and explaining the advertisement you have devised.

# Unit Three | Television

## Introduction

Television has become a hugely popular form of the mass media. To be able to transmit words and images into people's homes was a dream for well over a century.

This unit explores the way that programmes are made, the way language is used on television, and it gets you thinking about your own attitude towards television.

In this unit you will:
- gather research data and present it to other people
- learn about the variety of television presentation styles and formats, and look at the language used
- learn how information is presented
- look at the way soap operas are constructed and write the beginning of a soap opera.

## 3.1 Investigating television viewing patterns

### Objectives

- Find ways of researching information on television viewing habits.
- Present your findings to your group.

### Activity one

How much television do people in your class watch? Undertake a survey to find out answers to the questions below.
- How much television does your class watch **on average** per week?
- What is the longest and shortest amount of television viewing in your class?
- Which types of programmes are most popular in your age group (e.g. comedy, news, sports, etc?)

How will you approach the task? Use these guidelines to plan your approach:

1 Planning
- You could use a questionnaire or interviews to get the answers.
- What are the advantages of each approach?
- How would you organise interviews?
- How would you distribute the questionnaires?

2 Collecting data
- What format do you want the answers in – words, multi-choice responses, numbers?

Look at the two possibilities on the next page.

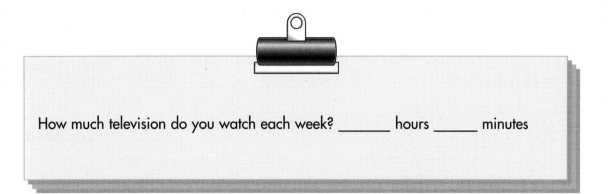

How much television do you watch each week? _____ hours _____ minutes

OR

How much television do you watch each week?

Tick one:

| | | | |
|---|---|---|---|
| Less than one hour | ☐ | 11–15 hours | ☐ |
| 1–5 hours | ☐ | 16–20 hours | ☐ |
| 6–10 hours | ☐ | More than 20 hours | ☐ |

Which format will make it easiest for you to compare results?
How will you collect the data?

 More information and guidelines on carrying out a TV survey are available from our website, www.heinemann.co.uk/devmediaskills.

## Activity two

Think of a format for showing your results most clearly.

Plan a presentation to the rest of your class to show what you found out.
This might include:
- using a poster
- a handout
- a PowerPoint presentation
- overhead projection sheets
- video report.

Plan who will speak and what they will say. Practise the presentation so that you are not relying on notes.

## Assignment

Read the report below about television viewing. Undertake a quick survey of people in your tutor group or at home. Choose a sample of five or more people to interview.

Use the questions surrounding the report to ask them three questions. Make a note of their answers. How far do their responses agree with the results of this report?

### TV: part of the family

Many people now organise their whole life around what's on TV. The television set is regarded like a member of the typical British household, according to a new survey.

75% of people arrange their living room furniture around the TV set, with 47% of people switching on their sets automatically when they get home.

The poll also found just over 33% of people build their meal-times around their favourite shows.

Soap operas are still the country's favourite programmes. *EastEnders* is voted the top show by most groups of viewers, except people over 50 in the north of England, who preferred Coronation Street.

In the survey 95% of people said that they thought television was entertaining and 91% found it educational.

1 What % of people in **your** survey do this?

2 Is it the same in **your** sample?

3 Do **your** interviewees agree?

Compare your survey results with other people's in the next lesson. Were they similar? What does this tell us about viewing habits? Present your results to the class.

# 3.2 Exploring television presentation styles

From the early days of television, presenters have talked directly to the camera as if they were speaking directly to each of us in our own homes. This is a technique you do not find so often in films, and yet on TV we treat it as entirely natural.

**A** Blue Peter team –
Christopher Trace, Leila Williams

**C** Andy Crane

**B** John Craven

## Activity one

Below is a tapescript of an ITV weather forecast presented by Sian Lloyd. Read through the extract carefully. As you do so, think about how the weather is presented on television.

### Tapescript

**Sian Lloyd:** Hello, good evening. Well, we've still got some heavy and thundery showers rumbling around, swirling around this area of low pressure, in turn sinking southwards over the next day or so, confining the heaviest of the showers to England and Wales. And the good news is for the north-west: fewer showers, more in the way of sunshine. A map of this radar picture from earlier today shows a good sprinkling of showers, some of those heavy – and even thundery in nature. And tonight those prove very reluctant indeed to fade away, especially down the North Sea coast. Elsewhere it becomes dry, but with some mist patches floating around. Early morning mist soon burns away tomorrow morning and it's a dry, bright start in a fair few places, already, though, that cloud tending to build up and we see a few showers cropping up. Then, just like today, those showers become a lot more widespread and frequent, heavy, even thundery in nature, especially so in central as well as eastern areas, but we can't rule out the odd heavy shower for north-west England as well as southern Scotland. As for the rest of Scotland – a lot of dry and bright weather, and the same goes for Northern Ireland. With our temperatures, then, at best 21°c or 70°f in the Southampton area, but a breezy day with it, especially later on, on the eastern side of the country. That's all from me, here's our weather summary.

**Voiceover:** Sponsored by Powergen, producing electricity, whatever the weather.

**1** Work with a partner. One of you is the presenter, the other the viewer. The presenter should present the weather forecast to the viewer as if speaking into a camera.

**2** Experiment with delivering it in different styles. The 'viewer' could suggest a style at random and the presenter could change their style to match. Try to do it without laughing. Here are the kinds of styles you might try out:
- smiling
- grumpy
- aggressive
- bored.

**3** Now experiment with a different type of presentation. What if the weather was not delivered directly to camera but instead was presented through an interview format?

Use the following as a starting-point and experiment with an interview style for telling viewers about the weather:

A: *Good evening, and here to tell us more about tomorrow's weather is* <u>*B's name*</u>

B: *Thanks, hi there* <u>*A's name*</u>

A: *Well, a day of heavy and thundery showers today. What's been going on?*

B: *You're right ....*

Present your interview to the rest of the class.

**4** What happens if you make the style of the transcript much more formal? At the moment Sian Lloyd's language is quite informal because of the features shown in the table opposite.

See what happens when you change those features and make the text more formal. The first part is rewritten below to get you started. Continue to redraft it so that you change the style of the whole text. Try to change the features in the table opposite: for example, choose formal vocabulary, remove fillers and reduce connectives.

| Feature | Example |
|---|---|
| Phatic language (greetings) | Hello<br>Good evening<br>That's all from me |
| Fillers | Well |
| Elisions | We've instead of we have<br>That's instead of that is |
| Lots of connectives | And<br>Or |
| Informal vocabulary | Rumbling around<br>Good sprinkling<br>Fair few places |

> We have still got some heavy and thundery showers present, moving around this area of low pressure. They will move southwards over the next two days, confining the heaviest showers to England and Wales. The news is more positive for the north-west ...

 This assignment is also available on our website, www.heinemann.co.uk/devmediaskills.

**5** Evaluate the effect of your rewritten version:
  **a** Does the weather forecast now seem more formal when you read it aloud?
  **b** Which feature makes the biggest difference to whether the text seems formal or informal?
  **c** What would you do to make television weather more informative?
  **d** Do you think it needs a presenter?

## Activity two

Television uses a huge range of presentation styles, from very formal to very informal. This means that the way presenters dress and speak will be different. In some programmes presenters will wear casual clothes. They will use informal language such as: 'Hi there ... today we'll be looking at ...'. In other programmes a presenter might wear a suit and tie, and use more formal language, like this: 'Good evening. On today's programme we will be hearing from ...'

Look at the list of programme types below. Which do you think would use the **most** formal style of language? Which would use the most informal language?

Use a scale like this one to try to place each programme:

Informal  1 ——— 2 ——— 3 ——— 4 ——— 5  formal

| | Programme | Scale 1 – 5 |
|---|---|---|
| a) | Wildlife documentary | |
| b) | Saturday morning children's programme | |
| c) | Chart music programme | |
| d) | Political interview | |
| e) | Comedy show for 20 year olds | |
| f) | Local news programme | |

 You can download this grid from the website, www.heinemann.co.uk/devmediaskills.

Compare your decisions with other people in your group. How did you decide which programme to place where on the grid?

## Activity three

The following is a script from a TV programme aimed at a young audience. Work in pairs and read the script – one of you as Tom, the other as Sasha.

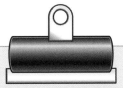

ITEM 16: **TRAIL** AHEAD
TOM **IN VIS** (STAIRS)

**SASHA:** Thank you Tom and don't forget we'll be talking about Eminem's UK tour later in the programme. Love him or hate him, you can't ignore America's first white rap superstar. The music press has praised his new album, but others feel that the

Trail: (trailer) a commercial for an item later on in the programme
In vis: in vision

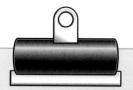

**ASTON**
EMINEM: LOVE HIM OR HATE
HIM? 0800 233233

controversial rap star should be
banned. So what do you think? Are his
lyrics harmless, or does the new bad
boy of rap go too far?

The number to call to register your
vote is 0800 222333 and everyone
who rings will be entered in to the
draw to win this week's top twenty
albums.

TAKE **VT** (INTO BREAK)

After the break, there's more from
this week's guest movie reviewer, Chloe
Rogers.

\* BREAK \*

ITEM 17: INTO BREAK
TAKE VT (INTO BREAK)
AND RUN SOUND OVER
THE END OF ITEM 16
STARTS ON MUSIC
ENDS ON MUSIC
**TC** IN 19:13:00:00
TC OUT 19:13:10:00
DUR 0.10

ITEM 18: OUT OF BREAK
STARTS ON MUSIC
ENDS ON MUSIC
TC IN 19:15:00:00
TC OUT 19:15:17:00
DUR 0.17

ITEM 19: TRAIL AHEAD
TOM IN VIS (SOFA)

**TOM:** Welcome back to The Mix! ...
Coming up – this week's guest movie
reviewer, Chloe Rogers. Also – our big
debate.

SASHA IN VIS (SOFA)

**SASHA:** Yes – Eminem – a talented
new face on the music scene, or an
offensive idiot?

TOM IN VIS (SOFA)

**TOM:** That's enough of that!

**ASTON**
EMINEM: LOVE HIM OR HATE
HIM? 0800 222333

**SASHA:** We want to know what you

**Aston:** device for putting graphics/labels on screen
**VT:** videotape
**TC:** timing cue

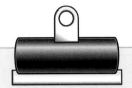

think and the phone lines are still open for you to cast your vote. The number to call is 0800 222333.

TOM IN VIS (SOFA)

**TOM:** And to make it worth your while to call, we'll even enter you in to our draw to win the week's top twenty albums.

ITEM 20: MOVIE REVIEW
SASHA IN VIS (SOFA)

**SASHA:** Now though we're heading over to Chloe Rogers, a school student from Suffolk, who's got the dubious honour of being our guest movie reviewer this week. Over to you, Chloe.

\* VT \*

ITEM 21: MOVIE REVIEW
TAKE VT
IN – CLAPPERBOARD SIGN
OUT – CHLOE SAYS "SEE YOU LATER"
TC IN 19.20.00
TC OUT 19.24.47
DUR 4.47

ITEM 22: ALT. PROSP.2
SASHA IN VIS (SOFA)

**SASHA:** Well, she's quite obviously not a Tom Cruise fan! Thanks a lot, Chloe.

ITEM 23: DEBATE
LINK
SASHA IN VIS (FLOOR)

**SASHA:** More from Chloe later on but now we're going to kick off our great debate for this week. Rap music's been around for a few years, but suddenly it's caused quite a stir. There's a new kid on the block and he's white, foul-mouthed and – depending how you look at him – a genius or a yob. What do you think? Should we admire Eminem or just ignore him? Phone in now with your point of view. We're looking forward to seeing what you think and we'll give the results later in the show.

## Activity four

How do you think the sequence from the programme should look on screen? Discuss:
- what the set should look like (use a sketch if you wish)
- how the presenters should be dressed, and why this is important
- how the presenters should stand, sit, how much they should smile, whether they should be talking direct to the camera or – at times – to each other.

## Activity five

What if the programme were a more serious news programme? How would you change the set, the dress of the presenters and their style of presentation?

Would you:
- sit them at desks?
- dress them in shirts and ties?
- change the script to make it more formal?
- even if you kept the same topics, how might you approach them differently?

Role-play the same sequence in a more formal style as if it was part of a news programme. Then perform your role-play to another pair or group. Ask them for feedback on how you changed the style of your language to match the more formal context.

Your viewers could use this checklist to notice ways in which you have made your language more formal:

| Text level | 1 How do the presenters organise their ideas – are they logical and clear? Do they use discourse markers (later, and now, next) to structure their speech? | ☐ Yes ☐ No |
| | 2 Does their language feel closer to written than spoken language at some times? | ☐ Yes ☐ No |
| Sentence level | 3 Do they use a range of sentences, or are most sentences co-ordinated with 'and' and 'but', making it closer to conversation? | ☐ Yes ☐ No |
| Word level | 4 Do they use more formal vocabulary? | ☐ Yes ☐ No |
| | 5 Do they use very little phatic language (e.g. hi, thanks)? | ☐ Yes ☐ No |

## Assignment

 This assignment is also available on our website, www.heinemann.co.uk/devmediaskills.

Some programmes have stopped using live presenters – they just use voice-overs and on-screen words. Undertake some research into which programme types use live presenters. Use a chart like the one below to sample as many programmes as you can this evening or over a weekend. For each one note down:

**a** whether or not a presenter is used

**b** some notes about the presenter's style

| Type of programme | Presenter used? | Formal or informal style? (think of where they are sitting, how they dress, their language) | Presenter needed? Why/ why not? |
|---|---|---|---|
| 1 Weather | ☐ Yes ☐ No | | |
| 2 News | ☐ Yes ☐ No | | |
| 3 Children's television | ☐ Yes ☐ No | | |
| 4 Documentary about computers | ☐ Yes ☐ No | | |
| 5 Youth magazine programme, like *The Priory* | ☐ Yes ☐ No | | |
| 6 Quiz show | ☐ Yes ☐ No | | |
| 7 Wildlife show | ☐ Yes ☐ No | | |
| 8 Film review show | ☐ Yes ☐ No | | |
| * | | | |
| * | | | |

*add your own categories here

**c** why you think the presenter is or is not needed.

Then give your response to the following questions.

**1** What type of programme do you think **needs** live presenters?

**2** Which work just as well without?

**3** Why are some programmes more formal than others?

# 3.3 Exploring television formats

## Objectives

- Evaluate how information is presented.
- Explore the style and conventions of some television formats.

Television uses images as well as words to entertain and inform us. Some people say that the images have a more important impact than the words – especially in news reports.

## Activity one

Look at this collection of images showing how the look of the BBC News has changed over the years.

1 Put the images in order of oldest to most recent. Discuss how you are making your decisions.

2 For each image, what do you notice about:
   - the way the presenter is dressed
   - the appearance of the news studio.

3 Even though the set design changes, do you think the basic format of the BBC news has remained the same?

## Activity two

The format of television news usually follows this pattern:
- headlines
- main presenter – introduces main story
- filmed report
- main presenter – either interview or next story.

Comedian Victoria Wood made fun of the format in her TV series *Victoria Wood – As Seen on TV*. In pairs read through this script of 'Reports Local'.

Reports Local

(Serious man at news desk.)

**Man**   And here in our area rioting and unrest continues in the town centre. Earlier today we had reports of windows being smashed and cars overturned. Our reporter Sally Hardcastle is down there now with a film crew to bring us this report.

(Pause – He listens to his earpiece.)

I'm sorry – the film crew are still having their lunch – there's been some delay with the moussaka at The Grill and Griddle. Sally Hardcastle is phoning in this report from the scene of the troubles.

(Flash up old school photo with Sally's face circled. He picks up his phone.)

What's the situation now, Sally?

(Sound of pips.)

Hello? What's the situation now?

**Sally**   (Voice Over) Hello? Is that the television studios?

**Man**   Yes, go ahead, Sally.

**Sally**   Could you put me through to Studio Three, please, I've got a report for Desmond Hambley.

**Man**   This is Desmond, you're on the air – go ahead.

**Sally**   Oh hello, Desmond, I didn't recognize your voice – I didn't think we've spoken on the phone before.

**Man**   What's the news on the riot, Sally?

**Sally**   I've spoken to your wife, haven't I, about that buggy? (Pips) Hang on.

**Man**   Are you in the middle of the danger area? It sounds pretty noisy.

**Sally**   No, I'm in Lewis's. I'm in a booth on the second floor, near the Travel Agents'. The noise you can hear is coming from the cafeteria.

(A picture comes up of Sally on the phone, a couple of people waiting behind her.)

**Man**   Ah, we have your picture now.

**Sally**   Yes, John's turned up, but Dennis is still waiting for his pudding. No, we came away from the rioting because it was so noisy.

**Man**   Is the situation deteriorating?

**Sally**   Well, as I said, we came away because it was looking a bit nasty. I was worried about my Renault ...

**Man**   Are the police planning to move in?

**Sally**   Well, I haven't really seen any police – lunch took ages, I had to send my chicken back, it was practically pink, then I looked round the sales, so ...

**Man**   Have there been any casualties?

**Sally**   Look, I don't know, I can't really talk now – there's a lady been waiting for ages, and I haven't got any more change – look, I'll pop back to the studios later, shall I? We'll probably have to make a detour because of this awful riot, have you heard about it? Anyway, look, Sally Hardcastle, for Local News, Lewis's, second floor, near the Travel Agents'. Bye!

(End on Man's face.)

1  In what ways does the script feel like a real news report?

2  How does Victoria Wood make us laugh at the format?

3  Look at the way the presenter in the studio (Man) speaks. Compare his language with the reporter's (Sally). Find three or more ways in which they speak differently.

## Assignment

Write your own parody (send-up) of a news programme. Use the format of a news programme you know well – either a national or local one. Start with the headlines and introduce the first story. To make the script entertaining you could either:

• use an unexpected main story ('The headlines: Toppers Fish and Chip Restaurant in Southwold has today introduced a new menu. Here, reporting from Southwold, is our correspondent, Jake Smith ...')

• imagine something goes wrong (the reporter can't hear; the wrong video is shown).

Video your news clip, or present it to the rest of your class as a piece of drama.

# 3.4 Studying Soaps

## Objectives

- Experiment with different ways of structuring and retelling stories.
- Explore standard English and dialect forms.

Soap operas are one of the most popular types of programme on television in the UK and around the world. Why do they have so much appeal?

In the 1800s, people eagerly waited the next instalments of novels by writers such as Charles Dickens. Like modern soap operas, his books had a wide range of characters, several storylines taking place at once and lots of dramatic moments to keep people wanting to know what will happen next. Today we watch soap operas, such as *EastEnders*.

## Activity one

Read the questions and answers opposite, from the BBC *EastEnders* website, to see how the programme is written.

**How do your writers come up with and research the major storylines?**

The Storyliners work closely with the Researchers when mapping out ideas for each storyline. When a story concerns a topical issue, e.g. Mark's HIV, as much information as possible is gathered from charities and doctors etc. This is then given to the writer so that they have all the details they need to write an accurate story.

 **How far in advance are the stories written for the show?**

Storylines are thought of and mapped out about six months before they are due to start filming.

 **Do you ever take storyline ideas from members of the public?**

No. Storylines are thought of and written far in advance and due to copyright laws we have to make sure they are all BBC-owned ideas and written by accredited writers.

 **I'm a professional writer. How do I get to write for *EastEnders*?**

In the first instance, you should send an original script (not based on *EastEnders*) of approx. 30 minutes duration to the script department. Your script should be emotionally driven, and contain more than one storyline.

 **How do you choose the background music for the pub and cafe?**

We research which songs are due out by the time the episode is due to be transmitted and get advance copies of music from record companies so we know what is going to be in the charts and likely to be played on radios and in pubs.

1 Notice that the answers refer to three different writing roles:
 • storyliners
 • researchers
 • writers.
 What do you think each role might be? How might they work together?

2 Look again at the advice for professional writers. What do you think it means by saying your script should be 'emotionally driven'?

## Activity two

Soap operas often contain the ingredients outlined below. For each one, see whether you can think of an example from a soap opera you know:

| Ingredient | Explanation | Example? |
|---|---|---|
| Cliffhangers | Ending each episode at a moment of crisis to make us want to watch next time | |
| Multiple narratives | More than one storyline going on at once | |
| Casting rosters | Some characters not in the programme in some episodes (because the actor is taking a break that week) | |
| Stereotypes | Villain<br>Heart of gold<br>Worrier | |
| Key locations | E.g. pub, café – places where people are likely to meet | |

## Assignment

**Single soap study**

Use a table like the one below to look at one soap opera in more detail. Try and video the programme so that you can stop and start it.

Watch the first five minutes and make notes. Try to be quite precise in only basing your questions on the first five minutes. Divide the soap opera into scenes, noting down what happens in each (see the table below).

 This assignment is also available on our website, www.heinemann.co.uk/devmediaskills.

Name of soap opera:

Date of episode:

**Scene 1**
Location:
Characters:
Dialogue: yes/no
What happens (1 sentence):
Length of scene:

Use your information to compare your chosen soap opera with others. You should be able to answer these questions:

1 which soap opera has the shortest/longest scenes?

2 which scene overall was the shortest?

3 how many scenes use no dialogue?

4 what different locations are used?

5 which soaps have the most dramatic storylines at the start of an episode?

# Extended Assignments

## Speaking and listening

A recent survey showed that many young people from the age of around 11 have their own television in their bedroom. Many also have videos.

Some people think this is wrong – that it is bad for young people to have such easy access to television.

What are the arguments for and against televisions in young people's bedrooms? Have a classroom debate.

## Writing

1 Use the list of soap opera ingredients on page 74 to create a soap opera based at your school. Brainstorm ideas for your new soap and then present them to the rest of your class.

   For example, think of:
   • a name for the soap opera
   • a storyline that leads to a first cliffhanger
   • three narratives for the first episode
   • your characters (five or six?)
   • key locations for different scenes.

2 Write the opening sequence of the first episode. Start it in the middle of some action – people discussing something that has just happened or is about to happen. Then cut to the next scene …

## Reading

It is hard to imagine a world without television. If films were the most important entertainment form in the first half of the twentieth century, television came to dominate the second half.

Read the article on the next page that explains how it all started. It is taken from a book about the history of television.

# *Who Invented Television?*

On 27 June 1923 *The Times* of London carried the following advertisement: 'Seeing by wireless. Inventor of apparatus wishes to hear from someone who will assist (not financially) in making working model. Write Box S. 686.'

The man lurking behind this box number was John Logie Baird. Within two-and-a-half years he moved from the personal column to the news pages: on 28 January 1926 *The Times* reported that 'Members of the Royal Institution and other visitors to a laboratory in an upper room in Frith-street, Soho, on Tuesday saw a demonstration of an apparatus invented by J.L. Baird, who claims to have solved the problem of television.' Noting that the image as transmitted was 'faint and often blurred', the newspaper commented: 'It has yet to be seen to what extent further developments will carry Mr Baird's

system towards practical use.' Ten years later, the British Broadcasting Corporation, in collaboration with Baird and EMI-Marconi, opened what was claimed to be the first regular 'high definition' television service in the world.

Baird's story is an engaging one, and it is no wonder that several generations of British schoolchildren have been taught that he 'invented' television. But he was not alone.

He was certainly not the first person to have had the idea of 'seeing at a distance'. In 1879, George du Maurier drew a cartoon for *Punch* which showed a mother and father watching, on the wall of their English home, a tennis match in Ceylon in which their daughter was playing. They were also able to speak to her, over a long-distance telephone.

In 1882, six years before Baird was born, the French artist Robida produced an even more startling series of drawings, in which moving pictures were transmitted on to the walls of people's living rooms. One of the screens showed a teacher giving a mathematics lesson; another showed a dressmaker displaying his wares (a prediction of 'shopping by television' a century before it became reality); another had a ballet being performed; and yet another showed a full-scale desert war being fought, while the viewers gazed in horror from their comfortable chairs.

1  Why did John Logie Baird place an advertisement in the newspaper: what did he need?

2  What was the reaction of *The Times* newspaper to the first demonstration of television?

3  How had George du Maurier and Robida also begun to develop the idea of television?

4  Some people might say that we would be better off without television. Working on your own or in a small group, make a list of some of the positive and negative effects television has had. Use a table like the one below.

| Positive effects | Negative effects |
| --- | --- |
|  |  |
|  |  |
|  |  |
|  |  |
|  |  |

## Introduction

The number of people using the Internet is growing fast, and it has been estimated that a new website is produced every ten seconds. How is the Internet similar to other media forms such as newspapers and television? What is it better at providing?

This unit explores the way the Internet presents information and entertainment, and the way language is used on websites and email.

In this unit you will:
- look at and analyse the different features that websites use
- write your own website homepage
- evaluate the way information is presented.

# 4.1 Looking at websites

## Objectives

- Evaluate how information is presented on websites.
- Explore the form, layout and presentation of websites.

A website gives you the chance to tell readers about yourself, your product and services. But because there are so many sites on the Internet and it is so easy to click onto a different site, building a really strong web page takes skill.

## Activity one

Renee Kennedy works for a marketing company and has written a guide to producing a successful website.

Read her guide, on the opposite page. How many of her points do you agree with?

Use the questions below to think more about Renee Kennedy's advice.

1 Write down two or three points from Renee Kennedy's advice which you strongly **agree** with. Why?

2 Write down anything you strongly **disagree** with. Why?

3 Which would you say is the most useful hint?

4 Which is the least useful hint?

5 Are there any points you think she leaves out of her guide?

# Five Secrets for Website Design Success
## by Renee Kennedy

## 1 AUDIENCE

You are trying to hook your readers – to get them to buy – because your product satisfies their most basic needs. For instance, they need your product because it's going to make them look and feel better about themselves.

## 2 GENERAL WRITING STRATEGIES

Visitors must have the ability to scan down the page and find what they want quickly.
Try the following techniques:

- *keep paragraphs limited to 2-4 sentences*
- *use headings*
- *use lists*
- *use bolds*
- *write it the way you would say it.*

## 3 PICTURES

I wasn't gonna say it but, 'A picture is worth a thousand...' You know the drill. And it's true!
If you have pictures of your product - include them. But download time must be considered.

## 4 GRAPHICS

Graphics can do good things for your site – but consider them very, very carefully.

### A Positives

- Graphics can create consistency – allowing your visitors to know they are at your site on every page.
- Graphics can aid in navigation – a button/background theme set will create consistency and help your visitors find all of your pages.
- Graphics can give your site a professional appearance which will help your credibility.

### B Negatives

- Graphics can annoy or confuse people – loud and flashy animation makes it difficult to read text.
- Graphics can slow your download time.
- Graphics can give the wrong message – do your graphics go with your products?

## 5 NAVIGATION

Navigation is how your visitors get around. If your visitors cannot find their way around – they are undoubtedly going to leave! Try these strategies:

- Your main directory should have a maximum of eight links.
- Organise your site in a hierarchical fashion – use a main directory and subdirectories if you need to.
- Don't underline text – unless it is a link.
- If you're creative – use graphics to make a 'navigational bar' or button links.
- Lay out your navigation on paper before implementing it on the web.

## Activity two

In her advice on writing style, Renee Kennedy lists different style features which can make a text more interesting – such as short paragraphs, headings, bold, and so on.

The text below is about young people's diets. How would you make it visually more interesting?

Use a photocopy of the text and mark on it how you would make it look more inviting to a reader. Plenty of room has been left around the text so that you can make comments and draw arrows.

Suggestions:
- decide where you will create new paragraphs
- think about using subheadings
- experiment with other format features – e.g. bold, underline, capitals, different fonts, styles and sizes.

Show your revised text to others in your class. Compare the way different people approached the task. Which was the most successful and why?

 This text is also available on our website, www.heinemann.co.uk/devmediaskills.

How young people eat

The diet of young people has changed a lot over the past fifty years. In the past we used to be worried about whether young people were getting all the right nutrients. Now the real concern is to make sure they receive a balanced diet. Some new research is quite disturbing. The main worry is that young people take very little exercise. Apart from children aged 4–6, about 50% of Britain's young people are mostly inactive. They spend less than an hour a day on physical activities. There's also a worry about fat intake. Young people consume about the same amount of fat as the recommended amounts for adults – but this is still higher than is healthy, especially saturated fats. It's also worrying that young people are not eating enough vegetables. The recommended intake is five different fruit and vegetables a day. On average British children are eating half that amount. Perhaps most worrying, 20% of 4–18 year olds eat no fruit in an average week. This means that they could be storing up some major problems for their future.

## Assignment

Examine the way two of the different websites below have been put together, using an evaluation table like the one on page 82. You can also apply the table to websites of your own choice. You could look at the links provided on the Heinemann Website: www.heinemann.co.uk/devmediaskills.

www.cats.org.uk/kitten.html

www.bhf.org.uk/

www.actionaid.org

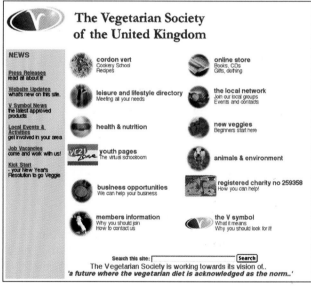

www.vegsoc.org

## Website evaluation frame

 To compare two websites copy the table below, or download it from our website, www.heinemann.co.uk/devmediaskills:

- make brief notes
- Give a rating: 1 = low; 5 = high.

| | Website 1 | Website 2 |
|---|---|---|
| **Audience** | | |
| Who do you think the audience is? | | |
| What age, gender, background do you think the audience is seen as having? | | |
| What clues are there in the language about the audience? | | |
| How well does the website address this target audience? Give examples | | |
| **Writing** | | |
| Is the writing style clear? | | |
| Are paragraphs short and easy to read? | | |
| Is the writing style informal or formal? How can you tell? | | |
| **Pictures** | | |
| Are pictures well-chosen? | | |
| How do they add to your interest in the site? | | |
| **Graphics (e.g. Headings/logos)** | | |
| Are graphics clear, eye-catching? Give examples | | |
| How do they make you want to read on? | | |
| **Navigation** | | |
| Is the site easy to move around? | | |
| Are links clearly signposted? | | |
| Are any parts confusing? | | |
| | | |
| **Best features:** | | |
| **Worst features:** | | |
| **Overall rating:** | | |

# 4.2 Designing a personal website

## Objectives

- Use a variety of techniques to organise and structure ideas.
- Write critically about media texts you have explored.

## Activity one

How would you plan a website of your own? Design a site using the guidelines below, together with the website design planner on page 85. If you have access to the software, you could even build your website once you've decided on a final version.

### Building a website

#### 1 Topic

Choose a topic. Choose something general so that you can add screens of more detailed information which readers can click on. For example, if your main topic is about yourself, then the sub-screens might cover topics such as:

- yourself
- school, e.g. general information – recent achievements – your class/ year group
- music, e.g. your different musical tastes – different groups – friends who play music.

Use a diagram like the one below to jot down your screens.

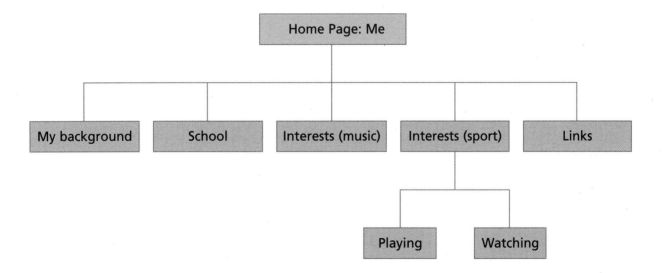

## 2 Audience

Identify whether you are writing for:

- your own age group
- older people
- friends
- strangers
- people who already know about your topics (less detail)
- people who don't know about your topics (more detail).

Discuss what differences these might make to the way you construct a website.

## 3 Purpose

Think about the purpose of your website. A website designed to persuade may have a different style from one which entertains. Use the checklist below to help you choose the most appropriate style.

### Style guide

Entertain

- Keep the text lively, light on the page, easy to read.
- Make the design style eye-catching, fun.

Inform

- Structure your information clearly – readers need to find their way around.
- Use short paragraphs, simple sentences, bullet points.
- Keep the design clear and simple.
- Use fonts, colour, text styles to inform and clarify.

Persuade

- Go for impact – grab your reader's attention with a slogan or headline.
- Keep your written style punchy, factual, and direct.
- Make the site attractive and bold.

## 4 Structure

Notice how a tree diagram such as the one on page 83 makes it easy to show the different levels of information you are including. Use a website planner like the one shown to plan the structure of your site. You can either copy it, or download it from our website. Take care not to make the site too complicated. Do a small amount well, rather than trying to do too much
at first.

## 5 Drafting

Use your planner to help you produce a draft of your home page. Write down the information you would like to include in your text boxes, so that you can practise getting the style right. Decide what kinds of images you would like to use. Show your draft to a friend and ask for their comments.

This activity is also available on our website, www.heinemann.co.uk/ devmediaskills. The website also contains a home page template that you could use when drafting your site.

# WEBSITE DESIGN PLANNER

**TOPIC:**

Purpose:
- to entertain
- to inform
- to persuade.

Firstly, think about the purpose of your home page. Are you writing just to interest people, to be informative or with a particular aim in mind?

**AUDIENCE:**

Identify whether you are writing for:
- your own age group
- older people
- friends
- strangers
- people who already know about your topics (less detail)
- people who don't know about your topics (more detail).

Think about your audience. The style of your home page will depend upon who you are writing it for.

**STRUCTURE:**

Title box – use this to help you decide what information the opening page of your site will contain.

**Notes**

Topic boxes. Use these to help you decide what kinds of topics you will cover on your website and where readers will have to click to find more information.

Sub-screen boxes. Use these to help you decide the content of each of your topic sub-screens. These should contain further information on the main topics you have decided to cover.

# 4.3 Handling information on a website

## Objectives

- Read and interpret information.
- Evaluate how information is presented.

## Assignment

Some websites suffer from having too much dense text on screen. They present information as if it were a page in a book. Practise editing information to make it clearer. Here are some of the techniques you might use:

- delete text
- make sentences shorter or longer
- add bullet points and/or subheadings
- use features such as bold, underline, italics to add clarity.

On the opposite page is a factsheet of information about bottlenose dolphins. Edit the text ready to place on a website informing 8–11 year olds about dolphins. The idea is to educate them as well as to entertain them. After reading your website, pupils should have learnt three or more facts about dolphin behaviour that they did not know before.

At the moment the information is very factual. It has a scientific tone. Your task is to make it easier for your target audience to read and understand. How would you edit the information?

- Which information would you delete (cut)?
- Which parts would you rewrite with simpler sentences and vocabulary?
- Which parts would you structure differently – for example, by shifting some sections to different screens?
- What design features would you add? (e.g. headings, bold, italic).
- Would you use photographs/images? (see page 88).

---

**Hints**
- Think of an attention-grabbing heading that will make readers want to find out more about bottlenose dolphins.
- How could you use bullet-points and lists to make the text easier to follow?
- What interactive features might you include (clicking on images or text to gain more detail? Interactive learning games?)?
- Choose what images you would want to include and where you would place them.
- What captions (labels) would you use with the images?
- How will you assess whether the pupils have learnt anything from looking at your site? Is there any activity you could build in where they have to test their knowledge and understanding?

# Bottlenose Dolphin Factsheet

A. Social structure.

1. Bottlenose dolphins live in groups called **pods**.
   a. A pod is a long-term social unit.
   b. The size of a pod varies. On the west coast of Florida, mean pod size is about seven animals.

2. In general, size of pods tend to increase with water depth and openness of habitat. This may be linked with feeding strategies and protection.

3. Several pods may join temporarily (for several minutes or hours) to form larger groups called herds. Up to several hundred animals have been observed travelling in one herd.

B. Social behaviour.

1. Dolphins in a pod appear to establish strong social bonds. Studies suggest that certain animals prefer association with each other and recognise each other after periods of separation. Mother–calf bonds are long-lasting.
2. Bottlenose dolphins establish and maintain dominance by biting, chasing, jaw-clapping, and smacking their tails on the water (Shane et al., 1986; Herman, 1980).
3. Dolphins often show aggression by scratching one another with their teeth, leaving superficial lacerations that soon heal (Shane et al., 1986). Traces of light parallel stripes remain on the skin of the dolphin. These marks have been seen in virtually all species of dolphins. Dolphins also show aggression by emitting bubble clouds from their blowholes.
4. During courtship, dolphins engage in head-butting and tooth-scratching.
5. Bottlenose dolphins often hunt together.
6. Dolphin courtship behaviour includes twisting, nuzzling, and tooth-scratching.

C. Daily activity cycles.

1. Observations indicate that dolphins undergo daily cycles of activity.
2. Bottlenose dolphins are active to some degree both day and night.
3. Social behaviour comprises a major portion of bottlenose dolphins' daily activities.
4. Feeding usually peaks in the early morning and late afternoon.

Below are four possible photographs that you could include on your bottlenose dolphin factsheet. If any, which of these images would you like to use? What captions would you use with the images?

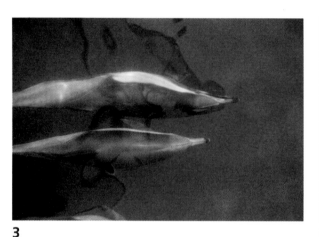

1

2

3

4

# Extended assignments

### Speaking and listening

Some people say that the Internet is exciting and full of opportunities for research, learning, interaction between people. Other people view it as dangerous.

1  What are the arguments for and against the Internet?

2  Do you think there should be controls on:
   • what is placed on the Internet?
   • whether everyone (including young children) should be given access to it?

3  Hold a small debate in your class concerning censorship of the Internet with some people taking one side, some the other.

# Reading and writing

## A  Website comparison

Choose a topic you are interested in, such as a sports team, issue or group. Write a detailed comparison of two websites on this topic. You could use the website grid on page 82 as a starting-point for your analysis. Then write up the results in a report using the structure suggested below.

In detail, discuss:
- the purpose (e.g. to inform the audience, entertain, persuade)
- the audience: who is it aimed at (age, gender, level of expertise)
- design (compare the layout – images, graphics, fonts, interactive features of the two sites)
- use of language (is it informal, chatty, easy to follow, technical?)
- ease of navigation (how easy is it to move around the site? Are links to other sites clearly marked?).

### Evaluation

Give your overall opinion of the two sites saying which you prefer and why.

> **Hints**
> - Keep your own writing style objective (or neutral) and factual, until the final paragraph where you are encouraged to give a personal opinion.
> - To keep the style formal, avoid using the personal pronouns 'I' and 'me' too often.
> - Support your ideas by giving examples from the site (e.g. examples of wording or design features). This will make your comparison more specific and more interesting for the reader.

## B  Email etiquette

What hints would you give to a new email user? You could give advice about:

- length of messages
- what tone to use (how formal or informal)
- how to reply (do you include the other person's message? Where?)
- using abbreviations (e.g. lol = lots of love)
- using lower case or capitals.

Design a poster of email advice.

 An activity on Internet language is available on our website, www.heinemann.co.uk/devmediaskills.

# Unit Five | **Newspapers**

## 5.1 Exploring newspaper layout

### Objectives

- Learn about how newspapers use layout.
- Look at newspaper designs from other countries.

To be successful, newspapers need to sell. They make their money from the number of copies they sell, and also from advertising. These two sources of income are connected: the more readers a newspaper has, the more they can charge for advertising. This is why newspaper layout is so important.

### Activity one

Imagine you are in a newsagent's shop, or at the news-stand in a station or airport. There might be more than 20 different news titles. How do you decide which newspaper to buy?

Look at this list of front-page layout features and decide which for you is **most** and **least** important:

- large front-page image
- big headline
- short paragraphs
- attractive newspaper logo (e.g. The *Sun*, The *Independent*)
- advert for something in the paper (e.g. 'Turn to page 22 for yesterday's sporting action').

Compare the different responses in your group.

- Do you all agree, disagree? If so why?
- Are layout features universal?

## Activity two

Why do you think newspapers use layout features such as headlines and columns? After all, you do not need headlines and columns to read a book.

Why do you think newspapers are not designed to look more like this?

1 This text now does not look like a newspaper. Which type of text does it remind you of?

2 Think of three reasons why newspapers are not designed to look like this.

## Activity three

Brainstorm what you already know about newspaper layout features. Map your ideas using a diagram like the one below. For example, you could make notes about the length of newspaper paragraphs, or the type of vocabulary used in headlines.

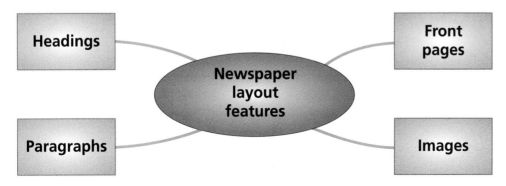

## Activity four

Explore the way different newspaper front pages are designed. Since the first newspapers were published back in the early seventeenth century, they have developed special layout features. Nowadays when we read a newspaper, we usually expect them to look like this:

The newspaper image is labelled with the following terms: Masthead, Headline, Byline, Subheadings, Columns (left side); Strapline, Pictures, Captions (right side).

**Daily Chronicle**

**TRAGIC DEATH OF YOUNG STAR**
*TV world in shock*

By Peter Jones

Emma Peterson in fatal accident

The world of television was left in a state of shock last night as news filtered through of the death of Emma Peterson, presenter of *You Want to Bet?*. Police confirmed that Ms Peterson had left Hollywoods, her favourite club, at about 2:30 am last night, after attending a charity event sponsored by her own television company, Azteq. Her husband, television executive Peter McCay, picked her up outside the club and then the couple drove towards their Bayswater home in McCay's blue BMW.

**Police investigation**

Detective Inspector Evans, who is leading the investigation, said that the accident occurred shortly afterwards, at the junction with Old Sarum Lane. The precise course of events is not clear, but it appears that the car collided with an oncoming lorry at considerable speed. Ms Peterson, who was apparently not wearing a seatbelt at the time, was pronounced dead on arrival at St Thomas' Hospital at 3:05 am.

McCay sustained serious spinal injuries and is currently said to be in a critical condition in St Thomas' Intensive Care unit. Police are anxious to speak to the driver of the lorry, thought to be a man in his early forties.

Friends of Ms Peterson are said to be 'horrified and appalled' at her death.

**Full story on page 2.**

Mourners lay flowers at site of accident

---

**Glossary**

**Byline:** tells you the name of the writer of the story

**Caption:** the text beneath a photograph saying what the image shows

**Headline:** the larger text that gives a taster of what the article is about

**Masthead:** the top section of a newspaper which contains its title, price, date, and often advertisements for items inside the newspaper

**Strapline:** the smaller headlines beneath the main headline. It usually adds detail to the headline

**Subheadings:** words placed between some paragraphs to signal the topic of the article

---

Using the terms above, compare the front pages of newspapers from three countries on the next page. Explore whether they all use the same layout features.

The newspapers were all bought in London on Wednesday 26 July 2000 – the day after the Concorde crashed on the outskirts of Paris. They come from France, Saudi Arabia and Germany.

**Al Hayat** (Saudi Arabia)

*Le Figaro* (France)

*Die Welt* (Germany)

1 To compare the layouts, decide what ratio there is of text/images/advertising (masthead and adverts) on each front page. Use the numbers 1 (least) to 5 (most), e.g.:

text: 5          image: 3          advertising: 2

Make sure the numbers add up to 10 so that you can give each feature a percentage. In this example the figures show that 50 per cent of the front page is text, 30 per cent is image and 20 per cent is advertising.

Estimate the ratios for each of the three front pages, using a grid like this:

|  | Le Figaro (France) | Al Hayat (Saudi Arabia) | Die Welt (Germany) |
|---|---|---|---|
| Text |  |  |  |
| Images |  |  |  |
| Advertising |  |  |  |

2 Which newspaper contains **most** different stories and which **fewest** different stories?

3 Which has the largest/smallest headline (font size)?

4 Which has the longest headline (number of letters)?

5 Which newspaper seems to devote most/least space to the Concorde story?

6 Which paper feels most similar to the design of a UK newspaper? Explain your answer.

## Assignment

Look at a newspaper from home, or one that your teacher has available in class. Use it to show your developing knowledge of newspaper design.

1 Sketch out the overall layout of the newspaper in the centre of a piece of paper.
2 Label the key features (masthead, headline, columns, and so on).
3 Estimate the ratio of text – image – advertising.
4 Write a paragraph saying what you like/dislike or find least/most successful and why.

 This assignment can also be read at our website, www.heinemann.co.uk/devmediaskills. The site contains links to other newspapers in the UK and around the world.

### Web assignment
Using the links, compare the layout of two front pages from different countries. Use a chart or table to show the similarities and differences.

# 5.2 Examining front page design

## Objectives

- Practise comparing newspaper layouts.
- Explore an example of poor newspaper design.
- Create your own newspaper front page.

Newspapers need to be eye-catching if they are to sell. Look at these essential layout ingredients of a modern British newspaper.

- Name of newspaper clear and in a memorable design style so that it seems different from other papers.
- Headline that attracts our attention – top half of paper so that we can read it even when the paper is folded in half or on a news-stand behind other papers.
- Interesting main image – again in the top half of paper.
- Information about what else is in the newspaper.
- Short blocks of text (paragraphs) so that we can read the story quickly.
- Occasional subheadings to help add visual interest to the page.
- Text arranged in columns so that more than one story can fit onto the page.

Now look at this example of a badly-designed front page.

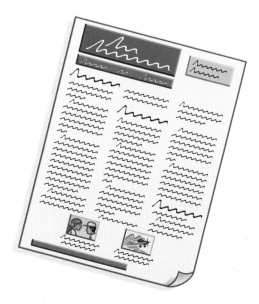

## Activity one

**1** Make a list of five or more faults you can see with the front page above.

**2** Is there anything you like about the layout?

## Activity two

1 Keep the same ingredients, but sketch out a design that you think is better. For example, move the pictures to better positions.

2 Then write a bullet-point list explaining the changes you made, like this:
   - picture moved to top half of page because …
   - headline …
   - text …

### Assignment

Imagine you are a newspaper design consultant. Write a memo to the newspaper editor saying what you think could be improved in the design on page 95. Use this example to get you started:

---

# SPENCER DESIGN CONSULTANTS

To:     A Walden, Editor, Daily News
From:   S Spencer, Newspaper Design Consultant

Date: _____

Amanda

As promised, I've just finished an analysis of the current design of the Daily News and I think there are plenty of things we could do to improve the way it looks. This should lead to readers finding it a more informative and more readable newspaper.

Here are my five main suggestions:

- 
- 
- 
- 
- 

I look forward to your comments.

*S Spencer*

---

**Web assignment**

How do newspapers design their online newspapers differently from their printed versions? Compare one title in its two forms, looking in detail at the balance of text, images and advertising. See the starting-points and links at www.heinemann.co.uk/devmediaskills.

# 5.3 Studying photojournalism

## Objectives

- Explore the power of images in newspapers.
- Learn about how picture editors make decisions about which images to use in newspapers.

Most newspapers use images as well as words to inform and entertain their readers. A picture can communicate the drama, shock, passion or excitement of an event that would take several hundred words to describe.

In an age before photographs, newspapers would employ illustrators to sketch pictures of the scene of a disaster, just as courtroom artists today capture the faces of those involved in the trial.

## Activity one

1 How important are photographs in newspapers? Do you think it would be possible to run a front page which did not have a photograph with it?

2 Are there times when using photographs is **not** justified? Look at the list below and decide what you think. Give reasons for your answers.

- Pictures taken of celebrities without their permission.
- Brutal pictures of people hurt or killed in war or violence.
- Page 3 semi-naked shots.

## Activity two

Danny John is executive picture editor at *The Guardian*. His role is to select the images which will accompany the articles. Here he describes what he looks for in a good photograph.

At the *Guardian*, we look for pictures that are different from the pack. I want an image which might take a normal subject but will show its subject in a manner which is out of the ordinary.

I aim to choose a photograph that harnesses all the skills of the photographer. She or he should take the idea concerned and show it in a way which is totally unexpected or give the impression that the subject has not been shot in that manner before.

The photograph will catch the eye immediately and stay with you all the way through to publication and, if possible, beyond.

This style will include the angle of the shot, the use of the light and the placement of the subject concerned.

A good photograph will never be dull and predictable in its presentation.

*Danny John*

Now take Danny John's ideas and apply them to the front page of *The Guardian*. On 24 July 2000, Concorde crashed. Here is *The Guardian's* headline and topic sentence from the main story:

# 113 dead in Concorde crash

July 25 2000

*An Air France Concorde has crashed outside Paris shortly after takeoff, killing all 109 passengers and crew on board the New York-bound flight.*

Look carefully at each of these images, similar to the ones that Danny John had to choose from.

**A**

**B**

**C**

**D**

**E**

**1** Start by looking again at the list of qualities
Danny John expects in a good photograph:

    **a** a picture that is different, out of the ordinary
    **b** an approach which is unexpected
    **c** a photograph which catches the eye immediately
    **d** a photograph which will stay with you
    **e** one which uses an unusual angle for the shot, or unusual use of the
       light and the placement of the subject concerned
    **f** one that is never dull and predictable in its presentation.

For photographs A–E, decide how far each contains these different
ingredients. To compare the photographs most easily, use a system like this:

Does not contain the ingredient = 0
Contains some of the ingredient = 1
Contains the ingredient = 3

| PHOTOGRAPH | Ingredient a) | Ingredient b) | Ingredient c) | Ingredient d) | Ingredient e) | Ingredient f) |
|---|---|---|---|---|---|---|
| A | | | | | | |
| B | | | | | | |
| C | | | | | | |
| D | | | | | | |
| E | | | | | | |

**2** Out of Danny John's list, which photograph is the most suitable for
the story?

**3** Which photograph would you use as the front page main image?

**4** Write a sentence to explain your choice.

## Assignment

Imagine you are a newspaper picture editor. The front page story in tomorrow's paper is new research about the health risks of mobile phones.

Here are four photographs you could choose from.
Write three paragraphs saying:

**a** which photograph you would use and why

**b** what caption you might put under the image

**c** what you look for in a good newspaper photograph.

**W** **Web assignment**
Use an online picture library (e.g. *Daily Mirror* library or Corbis) to find a better image to illustrate the mobile phone story. See the starting points at www.heinemann.co.uk/devmediaskills.

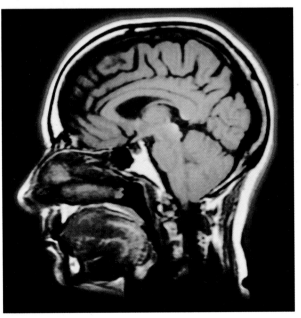

# 5.4 Exploring news stories

## Objectives

- Explore the way newspaper stories are structured.
- Learn more about the language of newspaper writing.

Newspapers contain a variety of types of writing:

### News stories

*Purpose:* to inform readers about events that happened the day before or (in an evening paper) earlier that day.

*Language style:* usually formal and less personal (for example the writer will not use the pronoun 'I').

### Features

*Purpose:* to inform and entertain. Features writing gives background information on news stories, or inform us about other topics, such as cooking, fashion, profiles of people, discussion of issues. They also include reviews of films and television programmes.

*Language style:* a huge range of language style is possible. Writing here will often include more personal styles.

### Opinion pieces

*Purpose:* to persuade. These express a view on a topic. The newspaper will have an opinion column (e.g. '*The Sun* Says …'; 'The Voice of the People'), stating its opinion on a major news story. This is sometimes called the leader column. Newspapers often employ columnists too – writers who give opinions in essays about a range of topics. Often these are designed to be controversial.

*Language style:* may be formal (e.g. newspaper opinion or 'leader' in a broadsheet newspaper), or informal (reader's letter expressing an opinion on the letters page).

| *Broadsheet newspaper* | *Tabloid newspaper* |
|---|---|
| Also sometimes called 'the quality press'. Large format newspapers that report news in depth, often with a serious tone and higher level language. News is dominated by national and international events, politics, business, with less emphasis on celebrities and gossip. Examples: the *Independent*, the *Guardian*, *The Times*, the *Telegraph*. | Smaller newspapers aimed at a large audience. News is reported in less depth and emphasises human interest stories. The language level is simpler, paragraphs and stories shorter, with more use of images. Content often includes more celebrities, media news and gossip. Examples: the *Sun*, the *Mail*, the *Mirror*, the *Express*. |

## Activity one

Use the following sentences to explore the language features of the three main types of newspaper writing. The sentences are all taken from one issue of *The Sunday Times*.

**1** For each sentence, decide whether it comes from:
   **a** a news story
   **b** a feature article
   **c** an opinion piece.

Use a chart like the one below to explain the main clue that helped you decide. As an example, the first one has been done for you.

**2** When you have completed the table, compare your answers with a friend's.
   • Which type of writing did you find **easiest** to identify? Say why.
   • Which type of writing did you find **hardest** to identify? Why.

---

**1** Last night the Automobile Association expressed concerns about Blair's latest initiative.

**2** Madonna Louise Veronic Cicone, as she was christened in Bay City, Michigan, has certainly lived a life colourful enough to have raised a few eyebrows.

**3** A group of scientists known in government circles as 'The X Files Committee' has warned that the Earth is overdue for an asteroid strike serious enough to wipe out 10 per cent of its population.

**4** Until world leaders start feeding themselves less and helping the world's poorest people more, many of the globe's neediest millions will stay trapped in a cycle of oppression.

---

| Sentence | News (n), features (f) or opinion (o) | Main clue(s) |
|---|---|---|
| 1 | News | • 'Last night' suggests a news story – something that has actually happened. <br>• Reference to 'Blair' – a real person <br>• Impersonal language (no I, me or you) makes it factual and informative, rather than an opinion |
| 2 | | |
| 3 | | |

## Activity two

Here are some word level features found in different types of newspaper writing. Work out in which type (news, features or opinion) you think each one is most likely to be used (some will occur in more than one type). Give a reason for each of your answers.

---

**Word level features**

1 Adverbials of place and time – e.g. yesterday, tomorrow, later.

2 Use of personal pronouns – e.g. I, we, you.

3 Use of past tense – e.g. said, commented.

4 Use of passive form – e.g. it was announced, it has been decided that.

5 Use of proper nouns – Blair, Michigan.

6 Use of abstract nouns – e.g. oppression, peace, evil.

---

## Activity three

News stories aim to tell you the whole story as quickly as possible. As the diagram below illustrates, newspaper articles often have a pyramid story structure.

**Headline**

Designed to catch your interest so that you want to read the story.

**Topic sentence**

The first sentence (sometimes printed in bold, or capitals, or a larger font) aims to give you the whole story in one go: who, what, where, why, when.

**Short paragraphs**

Newspaper stories start with the main events. Then they give more details and eyewitness comments in short paragraphs. The paragraphs at the end of the story are less important than those at the beginning. This allows sub-editors to shorten stories by cutting paragraphs from the end.

1 Now look at the way the writers of news stories use language to tell their stories. Read the story which appeared in the *Sun* on 25 July 2000.

2 If you needed to cut this story to make it shorter, which two paragraphs would you cut?

3 Are there problems if you simply cut the last two paragraphs?

4 Would the story still make sense after your changes?

# I GOT McDONALD'S SLAPPY MEAL

By ADAM LEE-POTTER

A MUM complained after waiting 15 MINUTES for her tot's McDonald's Happy Meal - then had it thrown in her face by an irate burger bar worker.

Anisa Sharkaoui claims the server also hurled her fish burger, six chicken nuggets, chips and large Coke over her as shocked customers looked on.

Furious Anisa, who retaliated by pouring a drink over the worker, says the man lashed out after she demanded a refund.

Police were called but said they were powerless to act in a 'civil matter'.

## Bun fight ... a McDonald's burger

Anisa, 25, who claims she suffered a grazed cheek, was offered a free ice cream after the bust-up. But she instead complained to McDonald's bosses.

The mum ordered the £1.99 meal for son Shakier, ten months, at her local branch in Notting Hill, West London.

She was told it would take five minutes, so she sat down to wait with the lad and three-year-old daughter Sara.

Anisa said: 'I wanted us to eat all together so I put our food to one side.

'But 15 minutes later the meal still hadn't come. I went to the counter and saw it sitting there. When I said they could have brought it to me as I had my hands full with two young children, they were really rude.

'So I took back our tray of untouched food and demanded a full refund. The man hurled it into the air, into my face.

'I'll never eat McDonald's again. I wanted a Happy Meal, but it turned into a Slappy Meal. I was treated like dirt.'

A McDonald's spokeswoman said: 'We're investigating the matter.'

*Annotations:*

- Headline uses a pun (word-play) to grab our attention: 'slappy' instead of 'happy'
- Topic sentence gives the whole story – who, what, where
- More detail about who and what happened
- More details about what happened next
- Sub-heading to keep the story moving
- More details about Anisa (eg her age)
- Background information and facts
- Comment
- Summary comment giving a different viewpoint

## Assignment

Look at the news story from *Metro* (29 June 2000), the free morning newspaper. It describes a parachute jump from one of Europe's toughest sites – the Eiger in Switzerland.

Here the paragraphs have been presented in a jumbled order.

1 Find the headline and the topic sentence. Then sequence the paragraphs in the order that you think they originally appeared in. Look out for **discourse markers** which help readers to see the way an article is structured. They can refer back to earlier information, or signal new topics. They include:
   • **pronouns** (e.g. he, they, it) linking back to a previous sentence;
   • **conjunctions** (e.g. but, after) linking one idea with another;
   • **adverbials** (e.g. afterwards, later) to organise ideas;
   • **linking phrases** (e.g. he added) to clarify the text.

2 Write down the three language clues that most helped you to unscramble the text. Compare your response with a friend's.

3 Write a short paragraph about how you approached this task. What did you find easy or difficult?

| A | 'I just said thank you to somebody, to something. Maybe it was the mountain I spoke with. Maybe nature.' |
|---|---|
| B | After 13 seconds of freefall, reaching speeds of 70mph, they opened their parachutes and landed at the base of the rock spire. |
| C | Some choose to leap from famous buildings, including the London Eye, Eiffel Tower, Moscow State University, the Christ figure in Rio de Janeiro and the 110-story New York World Trade Centre. |
| D | He rated the jump, his 30th, as the 'most impressive' yet. |
| E | Afterwards, Arch, 31, said: 'The moment the canopy opened, all the tension of my thoughts broke up. All the emotions came free and I could feel tears in my eyes.' |
| F | Where's the ripcord? |
| G | As part of the extreme sport of base jumping, enthusiasts are in a constant search for new platforms to leap from. |
| H | But the challenge for the sport is not to conquer the highest, or even smallest, jump-off point, but to experience extreme situations. |
| I | With the ground 6,000ft below and rapidly approaching, Hannes Arch from Austria achieved a world first. |
| J | 'We just like to push ourselves beyond the limit until we feel it has become really dangerous. I like to try and find my personal limit.' |
| K | He and fellow extreme sports enthusiast, Swiss Ueli Gegenschatz, 27, became the first to perform a base jump from the so-called Champignon, a mushroom-shaped tower rock formation on the north wall of the Eiger mountain in central Switzerland. |
| L | 'I like to pit myself against nature,' he said. 'We're not mad boys who risk our lives.' |
| M | But he added that it was less exciting than a previous exploit in which he leapt from a bridge just 650ft above a narrow valley which left almost no room to manoeuvre during landing. |

 To work on this on-screen, download this grid from www.heinemann.co.uk/devmediaskills.

# 5.5 Exploring fact and opinion in newspapers

## Objectives

- To look more at the language features of news, features and opinion writing.
- To spot differences between fact, opinion and bias.

We expect news reporting to be factual and objective, rather than subjective. This means we expect it to give us a neutral view, rather than the writer's personal opinion. Compare these two examples:

*Objective tone:*
- Suffolk school-teacher Matthew Taylor was yesterday awarded a medal for services to education.

*Subjective tone:*
- Suffolk schoolteacher Matthew Taylor, who used to teach me, was yesterday awarded a medal which he didn't really deserve if you ask me.

This is a very obvious example of the difference between objective and subjective writing. In real newspapers, it can be much harder to tell them apart.

## Activity 1

1 Look again at this sentence from the parachuting story on page 105.

> He and fellow extreme sports enthusiast, Swiss Ueli Gegenschatz, 27, became the first to perform a base jump from the so-called Champignon, a mushroom-shaped tower rock formation on the north wall of the Eiger mountain in central Switzerland.

   a What does the writer tell us about:
- **who** – age – nationality – background?
- **where** – detail?
- **what** they did?

   b What can you tell about the writer and the writer's attitude to the story?

2 Now compare an opinion piece. This is from an opinion column ('Voice of the Mirror', from the Daily Mirror). How is it different from a news article? As you read it, look out for examples of opinion and persuasion.

# VOICE OF THE MIRROR: GOING FOR GOLD

**THE world of sport is going stark raving mad.**

No sooner had we recovered from the news that Tiger Woods might earn £6 BILLION in his golf career than Portuguese soccer star Luis Figo is transferred for £40 million.

The sums of money involved are absurd, crazy and utterly indefensible. But it will never change, for one simple reason.

Ask any football fan in Britain if he'd mind his club paying £40 million for Figo and he'd say No. And ask any golf fan if they'd sell their house for a round with Tiger and they'd probably say Yes.

It's not sensible, it's just sport.

Use these prompts to explore the language of the text:

**a** News stories are usually factual. This opinion piece contains an opinion. What is it?

**b** News stories aim to be objective (neutral). The writer rarely refers to herself/himself using pronouns like I, me, us. Which personal pronoun does the writer use to refer to her/his own view?

**c** News stories might aim to use factual language and standard English. This opinion piece uses some informal slang terms. Write one down.

## Assignment

Using the information in the 'Voice of the Mirror' article, write the headline and opening sentence of a front page article about Luis Figo's possible transfer.

- Your headline should make readers want to read the story.
- Your topic sentence should tell readers who, what, where, when and why.
- Draw arrows to key language decisions you made in your headline and topic sentence. Explain the decision you made (e.g. tells the reader 'who'; active verb to add drama to the story …).

# Extended assignments

## Speaking and listening

In a small group, discuss these comments about photojournalism.

**1** See how far you agree or disagree with each opinion:

> 'Photographs have more impact than words.'
>
> 'In the UK a newspaper without photographs would probably not sell.'
>
> 'Taking photographs of people without their permission and then printing them is acceptable: it's what photojournalism is all about.'
>
> 'Topless photographs in newspapers should not be allowed because they have nothing to do with news.'

**2** Take one of the opinions and break it down into arguments for and against, using a two-column table.

**3** Number the arguments on each side to show which is strongest and which is weakest.

**4** Summarise the overall view of people in your group and present your shared opinion to the rest of the class.

## Reading

Read the article opposite from *The Daily Telegraph* and then answer the questions below.

## Comprehension

**1** What is the name of the child?

**2** How old was he when the accident occurred?

**3** In one sentence, say how the accident happened.

**4** Why do local people refer to it as a miracle?

**5** Write down three facts about the child's mother and three facts about his father.

## Language study

**1** Write down the topic sentence from the article.

**2** Look at the headline. If this were a front-page story in a tabloid newspaper (e.g. the *Mirror*, *Sun*, the *Express*, the *Daily Mail*, and so on), it might have a more dramatic headline. Write one down.

## Writing

**1** Write an opinion piece based on the 'baby in the ravine' story. Imagine you are writing in a tabloid newspaper and you want to make people aware of the dangers of winding mountain roads. Call for an inquiry into what happened and suggest more crash barriers. You might say also that it is good to be able to report news with a happy ending. Aim to write 200 words. Look back at the 'Voice of the Mirror' on page 107 to remind yourself of the style.

# Daily Telegraph

## Baby in car seat survives 300ft fall down ravine

**By Rosemary Behan**

**A BABY boy escaped with barely a scratch after falling 300ft down a ravine in the back of a runaway four-wheel-drive vehicle in France.**

Nigel Ryan, 40, and Claire Carter, 35, had stopped to take photographs next to the Pont de Terenez suspension bridge near Crozon in Brittany when their Isuzu Trooper careered down an embankment with their four-month-old son, Jasper, in the child-safety seat.

Mr Ryan, a graphic designer from Ardingly, West Sussex, said: "I was sure that he would be dead. We both were. It was simply the most terrifying experience of my life."

Miraculously, Jasper escaped with just a couple of scratches on his face.

"When I looked through the window and saw him looking at me I don't mind admitting that I burst into tears. It was a miracle," said Mr Ryan.

The vehicle, which was written off in the accident, was inches away from a river and had smoke pouring from the engine.

An investigation is underway into what went wrong. Mr Ryan said, "The handbrake was on when the Isuzu was at the top of the ravine, and it was still on when it was at the bottom."

Doctors have told Jasper's mother, Claire, a former managing direction of a PR firm, that it will take her son several weeks to recover fully from the shock of the accident.

She said: "Jasper's not settled at all. He's still crying and screaming, and he's not eating properly, which is unusual for such a young baby."

Mr Ryan called into a local church to light a candle just before the accident.

He said: "I think going into that church was a blessing in disguise.

"I only stopped off because my mother was always on at me to light candles in church.

"An hour later I was back in the same church thanking God for saving my son."

There have been several accidents at the Pont de Terenez, which the family had been visiting on a day trip, although no one is thought to have survived the drop before.

Locals were referring to the accident as "Le Miracle", said Mr Ryan.

2   Design your own newspaper front page.

You have two stories:

Story 1 – Major celebrity comes to your school to open a new building;

Story 2 – Fire at local fish and chip shop.

Your newspaper is local, and aims to be lively and appealing to a young audience.

Think of:

- a name for the paper
- a masthead (heading with paper title, date, price, advertisements for what's inside the paper)
- a layout which catches people's attention
- headlines
- topic sentences at the start of stories
- photographs.

# Unit Six | Comparing media

## Introduction

This unit enables you to compare texts in different media genres. It will help you build on your knowledge of how different media texts are written and why.

In this unit you will:
- look at how different media present the same topics and issues
- investigate and write about the structure, language and formality of different media texts
- look at the differences between texts which inform, entertain and persuade and at the differences between fact and opinion
- compare different media.

## 6.1–6.4 Comparing different media

### Objectives

- Look closely at the way media texts are written.
- Compare the styles and conventions of different texts.
- Write with clarity about what you have read.

This unit contains different types of media texts:

6.1 A) Advice on writing a radio play
   B) Extract from a radio play

6.2 A) Extract from a reference book: Michael Jackson
   B) Interview with Michael Johnson

6.3 A) Radio commentary
   B) Television commentary

6.4 A range of media texts about the *Titanic*
   A) Advertisement
   B) Message from the King
   C) Online profile of James Cameron, director of *Titanic*
   D) Front page of the *Daily Mirror*, 1912
   E) Review of the movie *Titanic*.

With your teacher, work through the different combinations of texts using the activities on pages 122–123 to help you analyse and compare the way different media texts are written.

# 6.1  Radio plays

Read the following extracts. With your teacher, use activities from pages 122–123 to compare the styles and conventions of these texts.

## A  Advice on writing a radio play

Have you ever noticed how difficult it is, in some films and TV plays, to work out who the people *are*? Is that his father the boy is talking to? Or his uncle? Or a friend, or the man next door? When the scene starts with two women, it may take quite a few minutes before you gather whether they are sisters or friends or whether they have just met.

In radio this can be even more difficult still—because the listener cannot even see the people. He only has voices to work from. For this reason, we must make sure—as soon as possible—to let the listener understand who the speakers are. You can do this in several ways.

- Use their names as soon as you can, and use them every now and then, later.

FATHER: I want to have a word with you, John.

JOHN:    I'm coming, Dad.

In all kinds of talk, you should remember to use this device of mentioning names. It will help to fix the people in the minds of your listeners. Don't forget that your listeners cannot see names like FATHER or JOHN in capital letters on your script. It's clear enough to you, and to people who *read* the script—but not to people who listen. They only hear what is spoken. By the way, you could try listening, any time, to the way people use the names of the persons they speak to. Some people do this a great deal; some don't. See how your teachers (and your friends) vary in this respect.

- Quite apart from names, it is important to make clear what your characters are to each other—What are their relationships? Are the two speakers husband and wife, or two sisters, or friends, or employer and employee, or teacher and student, or two strangers?

## B Extract from a radio play *Trouble on the Line* by Jennifer Hayes

*(The sound of coins inserted into phone box. Announcer's voice above continuing effects)*

Announcer Trouble on the line …
*(Madge and Lillian are sitting in Madge's living room having their tea. There is the sound of a telephone ringing in the room)*

Madge Don't answer it. It'll be a wrong number.

Lillian Why?

Madge It'll be a wrong number.
*(The ringing stops)*

Lillian It stopped sudden anyway. Didn't it stop sudden?

Madge That's just what I mean, there wasn't anybody there.

Lillian Not a genuine caller?

Madge No, they'd have held on longer.

Lillian It was sudden.

Madge As I was saying Lillian …

Lillian Before we were interrupted.

Madge Mrs Gramson. She was eating sardines in a bath bun.

Lillian Madge … no!

Madge She was.

Lillian She showed you?

Madge She made no attempt to hide it.

Lillian Madge, how did you know it was a wrong number just then as soon as the phone started ringing?

Madge I get so many. I know what to expect.

Lillian You could ring the operator.

Madge She wouldn't know anything about it.

Lillian You dial a hundred.

Madge I know you dial a hundred. I did the other night when the phone rang at half past twelve – that was last week.

Lillian I heard it ring late. What did she say?

Madge Who?

Lillian The operator when you rang her.

| | |
|---|---|
| *Madge* | It was a he, a very nice young man, very polite, he apologised. |
| *Lillian* | I suppose he had to. It's this new system they've installed. |
| *Madge* | That's what he said. |
| *Lillian* | Automatic … I knew it. |
| *Madge* | It tinkled all this morning. |
| *Lillian* | I didn't hear it. |
| *Madge* | On and off … on and off all the time. |
| *Lillian* | Did you pick the receiver up? |
| *Madge* | Yes. |
| *Lillian* | Who was it? |
| *Madge* | No one. |
| *Lillian* | Did you say anything? |
| *Madge* | I said 'Hello … hello.' There was no one there. |
| *Lillian* | Leastways you didn't think so. |
| *Madge* | No … I listened for breathing. |
| *Lillian* | They might have held their breath so … |
| *Madge* | And then I rang him. |
| *Lillian* | Who? |
| *Madge* | The operator. |
| *Lillian* | He doesn't mind you ringing often? |
| *Madge* | No, it was a she this time. She's very polite too … well educated. She said it was probably workmen. |

# 6.2 Personal record

Read the following extracts. With your teacher, use activities from pages 122–123 to compare the styles and conventions of these texts.

**A Entry from a music reference book about the early career of Michael Jackson**

### MICHAEL JACKSON
*b. 29 August 1958, Gary, Indiana, USA*

Former lead singer of the family group **The Jackson Five**, Michael Jackson's immaculate solo album *Thriller* became the biggest-selling record in music-industry history.

He first sang in public with his brothers at the age of six and began a solo career in 1971 in parallel with that of the group. *Got To Be There* produced hits with the title track and a revival of **Bobby Day's** 1958 song *'Rockin' Robin'*. The following year he reached the British Top Ten with **Bill Withers'** song 'Ain't No Sunshine' and had an American No. 1 with the sentimental film theme 'Ben'.

Further albums from this period – *Music and Me* (1974) and *Forever* (1975) – were hampered by Motown's giving their young star sub-standard romantic material and oldies like 'Too Young'. His only hit single during the mid-seventies was 'Just a Little Bit of You'. Michael Jackson's career only began to gain momentum after his appearance with **Diana Ross** in *The Wiz*, a remake of *The Wizard of Oz* starring black actors. While the film was a critical failure, its musical director was **Quincy Jones**, whose production of Jackson on the dynamic 'You Can't Win' signalled the beginning of a major partnership.

The first fruits of the Jackson–Jones collaboration were the five hit singles from *Off the Wall* (Epic, 1979). The album included the dance classics 'Don't Stop (Till You Get Enough)' and 'Rock with You' by **Heatwave**'s Rod Temperton (both million-sellers), as well as the slow ballad 'She's Out of My Life'. Jones' high-definition production was embellished with string orchestration and horn arrangements scored by Jerry Hey.

Motown capitalized on the revival of Jackson's career by re-releasing 'One Day in Your Life', which reached the British Top Ten in 1981, but Jackson underlined his pre-eminence as the most popular contemporary singer with *Thriller* (1982), whose title track was another Temperton composition.

## B Interview by Timothy White with Michael Jackson

**Q** *Are you hot for dance singles these days?*

**A** Yes. Both – ballads and dance singles. I just love to see the kids have a good time when the music comes on. Sometimes I sneak into this skating rink when they put them jams on. And you can tell when something's dirty: the kids be kicking in. Soon as there's something hot – ow! – they break out. Which is important, because people like to dance and have a good time.

**Q** *Speaking of ballads, I think back to the song Ben. Even though it was Number 1 in 1972, a lot of people don't know the song's about a rat. They haven't seen the film, so they see the song as a ballad about friendship.*

**A** Umm hmm. I like it both ways.

**Q** *How do you mean?*

**A** I mainly like it as a record. I love rats. And I like it as a friend, too, as if I'm talking to a guy that's a friend of mine – [*blushing smile*] but none other than just a friend! Some people see it the rat way. Some people see it the friend way. It works both ways.

**Q** *You're big on rats?*

**A** I love them. I used to raise them.

**Q** *White rats? You raised them at home?*

**A** Yeah. In cages and things.

**Q** *You've gotten out of it now?*

**A** [*Nodding*] You know, 'cause rats have weird characteristics. [*Very sheepishly*] They start eating one another. They really do. It just got sickening to me, and I just said forget it. I came home one night and looked in the cage, and the rats had started eating each other. The *father* was eating the babies. I got sick of looking at it all and left their cage outside. I didn't realize how cold it was. The rats, still alive, froze to death. [*Laughs*] I don't mind talking about it, if you don't. Do you?

Plus, in Beverly Hills there's a lot of snakes. I almost got bit by one rattlesnake because of the rats. See, when you live up in the hills, that's what happens.

**Q** *The rats draw snakes?*

**A** Umm hmm! Tremendously.

**Q** *And it was cold enough in Beverly Hills one night to freeze the rats?*

**A** Yeah, oh yeah. See, it's high *up*. There was a strange mist around, a rainy type of coldness, and the snakes started coming out of the ground to get the rats. I guess I got caught in the middle of this thing. It was awful! [*Laughs*]

**Q** *How many rats did you have?*

**A** Oh, I had quite a few. A lot of them. My mother hated it. I was up to about thirty rats.

# 6.3 Radio and television commentaries

Read the following extracts. With your teacher, use activities from pages 122–123 to compare the styles and conventions of these texts.

As you read, you will need to take notice of what the symbols mean.

## A Horse racing radio commentary

| | | |
|---|---|---|
| (.) micro pause | t. incomplete word | (1.0) pause in seconds |
| .h breath intake | :: elongated sound | *italic refers to the racehorse name* |

Away they break then (.) er *Black Snowfall* one of the last to break sits at the back of the field along with er *Tyne's Darling* who er has yet to settle (.) she's running very freely out the back and Johnny Murtagh will er t. (1.0) in fact she hasn't settled at all (.) he doesn't want to do too much too soon with her (.) or erm she might just use herself up very early on (.) running head strong like er a headless chicken (1.0) out the meanwhile is *Double Blessing* in the colours of the Queen (.) .h but turning for home its *Amies Lad* who has the advantage from *Rowan Rough* on the outside *Sea Bass* has got a good pitch on the fence with .h er Ted Suddaby *Moll Flanders* wider of those disputing thir::d (.) as they straighten then for home and er .h the Australian Graham Riley on *Take No Hostages* runs mid table wider is *Bring Assistance* running just on the inside er of that one (1.0) way back in the pack is *Open Mind* who is in centre field ahead of *Disraeli's Fortune* .h last but one *Tyne's Darling* (1.0) last of all *Send No Flowers* .h (.) at the back also is the Queen's runner *Double Blessing* .h so past half way and er turning to face the Judge and its er and there are four furlongs to run and er punched up the far side er *Bring Assistance* (.) still all to play for past the three furlong pole now (.) *Rowan Rough* and .h *Moll Flanders* and early leader *Rowan Rough* is dropping away through the field like er a stone through water .h *Candy Curls* makes good ground and er here comes *Tyne's Darling* with a big run the outside to join the leaders (1.0) the favourite strikes the front now .h er impressively moves on (.) .h *Double Blessing* is running on out of the pack and *Sea Bass* fills third possy the inside (.) into the final Quarter (of the final furlong)(.) has she gone too soon *Tyne's Darling* she's stopping in front and *Sea Bass* and Frankie Dettori begin to close (.) she's all over the place this leader *Tyne's Darling* holding on close home .h she's idling again wandering across the track(.)very gree::n (.) the favourite HOLDS ON (.) *Tyne's Darling* wins.

## B  Horse racing television commentary

| | | |
|---|---|---|
| (.) micro pause | t. incomplete word | (1.0) pause in seconds |
| .h breath intake | :: elongated sound | *italic refers to the racehorse name* |

They jump away then (.) white jacket *Bring Assistance* and er (.) beginning er a bit slow (1.0) was *Tyne's Darling* at the rear of the field settled at the back (1.0) up front on the outside *Rowan Rough* is one of the first to show with er *Amies Lad* running very freely indeed with *Sea Bass* (.) yellow jacket the ins::ide (1.0) out wider is *Moll Flanders* .h   in the green and white diamonds (.) followed by *Candy Curls* and *Black Snowfall* (1.0) caught up on the inside in the pink (.) back on the rail to *Open Mind* in the blue and white then *Bring Assistance* and *Tyne's Darling* .h towards the back .h at this stage (1.0) *Disraeli's Fortune* and er *Double Blessing* is just about last of all (1.0) they're running towards the turn at what seems to be a swinging pace here and it's *Amies Lad* (.) from *Rowan Rough* in second (.) *Moll Flanders* (.) *Sea Bass* back on the inside the::n .h followed by *Bring Assistance* (.) *Candy Curls* back on the fence (1.0) *Take No Hostages* out wider the purple and green halves .h then followed by *Open Mind* (.) *Tyne's Darling*  now moving forward with that big stride of her::s .h in the green colours of the Aga Khan (.) moving up effortlessly at this stage *Black Snowfall* is on the outside followed by *Double Blessing* and *Disraeli's Fortune* (.) they straighten up for home then .h *Rowan Rough* has taken over now from *Moll Flanders* (.) here comes *Tyne's Darling* on the outside *Candy Curls* back on the rail (.) *Take No Hostages Disraeli's Fortune* out deep (.) *Sea Bass* in the out wider *Black Snowfall* makes headway and *Double Blessing* is running on (1.0) .h the outside *Tyne's Darling* has gone on now (.) but she's looking about herself in front second *Candy Curls* (.) *Sea Bass* in the yellow (.) still *Tyne's Darling* from *Sea Bass* second now *Candy Curls* lies in third four is *Disraeli's Fortune* (.) furlong to go (.) *Bring Assistance* running on late the centre of the course (.) *Tyne's Darling* she's green (.) idling in front she's all over the shot (.) sways across *Sea Bass* but holds on to win the *May Hill*.

# 6.4 Special feature: the *Titanic*

Read the following five texts from different genres – texts with very different styles and purposes, all related to the sinking of the *Titanic*. With your teacher, use activities from pages 122–123 to compare the styles and conventions of these texts.

## A Advertisement for sailing from New York

**WHITE STAR LINE**
ROYAL & STEAMERS
UNITED STATES MAIL

FIRST SAILING OF THE LATEST ADDITION TO THE WHITE STAR FLEET

The Queen of the Ocean

# TITANIC

LENGTH 882½ FT.    OVER 45,000 TONS    BEAM 92½ FT.
TRIPLE-SCREWS

This, the Latest, Largest and Finest Steamer Afloat, will sail from
**WHITE STAR LINE, PIER 59 (North River), NEW YORK**

## Saturday, April 20th At 12 Noon

All passengers berthed in closed rooms containing 2, 4, or 6 berths, a large number equipped with washstands, etc.

THIRD CLASS FOUR BERTH ROOM
Spacious Dining Saloons
Smoking Room
Ladies' Reading Room
Covered Promenade

THIRD CLASS DINING SALOON

Reservations of Berths may be made direct with this Office or through any of our accredited Agents

THIRD CLASS RATES ARE:

| | |
|---|---|
| To PLYMOUTH, SOUTHAMPTON, LONDON, LIVERPOOL and GLASGOW. | $36.25 |
| To GOTHENBURG, MALMÖ, CHRISTIANIA, COPENHAGEN, ESBJERG, Etc. | 41.50 |
| To STOCKHOLM, ÁBO, HANGÖ, HELSINGFORS | 44.50 |
| To HAMBURG, BREMEN, ANTWERP, AMSTERDAM, ROTTERDAM, HAVRE, CHERBOURG. | 45.00 |

TURIN, $48.    NAPLES, $52.50.    PIRAEUS, $55.    BEYROUTH, $61., Etc., Etc.

DO NOT DELAY: Secure your tickets through the local Agents or direct from
**WHITE STAR LINE, 9 Broadway, New York**

## TICKETS FOR SALE HERE

## B Message from the Royal Family

# MESSAGE FROM THE KING.

## SYMPATHY WITH THE BEREAVED.

### TELEGRAM TO WHITE STAR LINE.

The White Star Line have received the following telegram from the King and Queen:—

Sandringham,
        Tuesday, 6.30 p.m.
The Managing Director,
    White Star Line,
        Liverpool.

The Queen and I are horrified at the appalling disaster which has happened to the Titanic and at the terrible loss of life.

We deeply sympathise with the bereaved relatives, and feel for them in their great sorrow with all our hearts.

GEORGE R.I.

Queen Alexandra telegraphed to the White Star Line:

Sandringham, Tuesday.
It is with feelings of the deepest sorrow that I hear of the terrible disaster to the Titanic and of the awful loss of life. My heart is full of grief and sympathy for the bereaved families of those who have perished.    ALEXANDRA.

**C  On-line profile of James Cameron, director of *Titanic* (from an entertainment news website)**

## James Cameron tells the astonishing story of *Titanic*, his breathtaking labour of love

By Rick Schultz

It's two weeks before the release of *Titanic*, and an enormous sense of relief is apparent on James Cameron's tightly drawn face. And why not? After three years of relentless toil, his $200 million gamble is no longer just the most expensive movie ever made – it's his favourite, and the critics seem to like it as much as he does.

Suddenly, nobody seems to care whether *Titanic* will earn its money back. Cameron, the acclaimed action auteur of *Aliens*, *True Lies*, and the *Terminator* movies, has used modern special effects technology in the service of good old-fashioned storytelling to make something new out of the best-known disaster tale of the century. Leonardo DiCaprio and Kate Winslet star as lovers aboard the 'unsinkable' British luxury liner that collided with an iceberg in the North Atlantic early on the morning of April 15, 1912. The *Titanic* – lovingly and painstakingly recreated in the film – sank two hours later, and more than 1,500 of its 2,200 passengers died.

Cameron, 43, actually backed into the *Titanic* story a decade ago. While researching deep-sea submersible systems for his film *The Abyss*, he met explorer Robert Ballard, leader of the crew that had recently located the *Titanic* wreckage off the coast of Newfoundland. Sufficiently inspired, Cameron took two deep-sea submersibles to the Atlantic floor in 1995, and brought back wrenching footage of the real *Titanic* wreckage that appears on-screen in the movie's present-day framing device. All told, he made twelve gruelling dives – many of them lasting fifteen to seventeen hours – and logged more hours on the *Titanic* than the passengers did back in 1912.

88.8%  Page: 1

**D Front page of the *Daily Mirror*, Friday 19 April 1912**

# The Daily Mirror

### THE MORNING JOURNAL WITH THE SECOND LARGEST NET SALE.

No. 2,648.    Registered at the G.P.O. as a Newspaper.    FRIDAY, APRIL 19, 1912    One Halfpenny.

## WHY WERE THERE ONLY TWENTY LIFEBOATS FOR 2,207 PEOPLE ON BOARD THE ILL-FATED TITANIC?

Something must be done by the Board of Trade to insist upon a larger number of lifeboats being provided for giant liners. Only twenty lifeboats were supplied by Messrs. Harland and Wolff for the Titanic, and even twenty, according to the Right Hon. A. M. Carlisle, the man who, as general manager to the company, was responsible for the building, was four in excess of the number required to comply with the Board of Trade regulations. "As ships grew bigger I was always in favour of increasing the lifeboat accommodation," said Mr. Carlisle, "yet it remains the same for a ship of 50,000 tons as for one of 10,000." The photograph shows the lifeboats on board the Titanic. It was taken while the giant liner was in Queenstown Harbour on Thursday of last week, in sight of land for the last time. Two boats, or even three if necessary, may be swung as easily as one on this type of davit. It will be seen that there is only one in the photograph.

## E Review of the movie, *Titanic*.

It is impossible not to be overwhelmed by the sheer scale of this film. The superlatives come thick and fast before you even enter the Southampton docks in the opening scenes – the most expensive film ever made, the biggest grossing film in history, the largest scale model ever used in a film. *Titanic* the film has mirrored *Titanic* the ship by entering into history, and as a reviewer it can be difficult to escape this. It is hard to be objective about a film which has so clearly captured the hearts and minds of such a vast number of people. It is also pointless to attempt to summarise the 194 minute plot, particularly as even those few of you who haven't seen the film will at least know the ending ...

Despite all this, there is no doubt that the film has its fair share of flaws. The awesome backdrop of history looming over the film leaves its mark on the characterisation of the main protagonists, Rose (played by Kate Winslet) and Jack (Leonardo Di Caprio). The scene is so vast that it takes the first two hours of the film just to set it, and this is often done rather clumsily – not all rich English girls were beautiful but unhappy, nor were all Irishmen charming yet lovable rogues with an excellent sense of rhythm. There is a very strong sense that these people are here simply to give us a focus, a window onto history, so that we can make sense on a human level of the chaos and terror that the last third of the film goes a long way towards conveying. The problem with this is that we end up with the worst of both worlds. The love-story gets in the way of the slow, terrifyingly inevitable unfolding of a genuinely tragic event, whilst the fact that everybody knows the final outcome mitigates what we can allow ourselves to feel for the characters involved.

Nevertheless, this is an ambitious work, witness to a genuine and all too rare attempt to make human sense out of events fixed resolutely outside human needs and desires. As such, its considerable failures must be considered as a greater achievement than many films which succeed on a much lower scale.

## Activity one

**Focus on content**
What are the texts about? Focus on the key words. Create a chart or table like the one below based on the following:
- Are the words familiar or more unusual?
- Are there technical words?
- Is there any non-standard vocabulary (words you would not expect to find in a dictionary)?
- Are the words simple or complex? (for example, count the syllables).
- Try replacing them with simpler or more complex words. What effect does it have on the text?
- What happens if you reduce the amount of description – for example by deleting adjectives and adverbs? What happens if you increase the description?

In your table leave yourself lots of space to add examples for each category.

| Words in text | Familiar/ unusual | Technical | Non- standard | Simple/ complex | Replacement words | Descriptive adjectives/ adverbs |
|---|---|---|---|---|---|---|
| Radio plays<br>A<br>B | | | | | | |
| Personal record<br>A<br>B | | | | | | |
| Commentaries<br>A<br>B | | | | | | |
| *Titanic*:<br>A<br>B<br>C<br>D | | | | | | |

## Activity two

**Focus on structure**
How are the texts structured?
- Do they use paragraphs?
- How long or short are the paragraphs?
- Is the text organised in a particular order? What would happen if you switched the order of paragraphs around?
- Does the first sentence of each paragraph give you a clue to what the paragraph is about?

Draw a diagram, chart or skeleton structure to show what the main idea is in each section or paragraph.

Now find the words which link these ideas together – pronouns such as: he, him, it; or discourse markers such as: also, after that, later.

## Activity three

**Focus on audience and purpose**
Compare the pair texts by making a two-column diagram. In each column write down everything you can work out about the audience for each text – e.g. age, gender, how much they already know about the subject.

Now do the same for purpose. What is the text intended for – to inform, entertain, persuade? How can you tell?

## Activity four

**Focus on style and formality**

**Style**
What do you notice about the writer's style in each extract?
- What kinds of words do you notice?
- What kinds of sentences do you notice?
- What can you tell about the writer's intended audience?

**Formality**
How formal or informal is each text?

Look at the sentences and vocabulary.
- Formal texts often use more complex sentences.
- Informal texts use vocabulary which is often familiar to us, less technical, and words may be shorter.
- Formal texts may use more formal discourse markers – such as 'on the other hand', 'however', 'therefore'.

Place the texts on a scale of formal to informal.

Rewrite the first part of each text using a different style. Then write a paragraph explaining how you have changed it.

## Activity five

**Focus on genre**
What is the genre (type) of each text?

Rewrite the first paragraph of an extract in a different genre – for example, rewrite an interview as a diary; a newspaper as a leaflet; a transcript as a formal report.

Then write a paragraph describing the effect of making this change.

# Glossary | Media terms

This glossary is designed to give you technical terms to help you write in more detail about media texts. It includes many of the terms used in television, film, newspapers and marketing.

| | |
|---|---|
| Biased | One-sided rather than neutral or objective |
| Broadsheet newspaper | Also sometimes called 'the quality press'. Large format newspapers that report news in depth, often with a serious tone and higher level language. News is dominated by national and international events, politics, business, with less emphasis on celebrities and gossip. Examples: the *Independent*, the *Guardian*, *The Times*, the *Telegraph* |
| Connotation | The feelings and thoughts we associate with a word, as opposed to the denotation which is its dictionary definition. The connotation of child might be 'innocent, vulnerable'. The denotation is 'young adult' |
| Denotation | The dictionary definition of a word |
| Disinformation | Giving incorrect information about a subject (it can be a polite term for telling lies) |
| Discourse markers | Words and phrases which help readers and listeners to follow the structure of a text. They can refer back to earlier information, or signal new topics. Look out for: 'earlier', 'later', 'in fact', 'however', 'meanwhile', 'despite this' |
| Fade | Type of camera effect: fade = the image moves to darkness |
| Dubbing | Adding a sound track to a sequence of images |
| Editorial | Newspaper articles giving the newspaper's opinions on the main stories of the day. They are also sometimes called 'leader articles' |
| Focus group | Group of people invited to comment on a new product or campaign. Researchers then use their comments to decide how best to market the product |
| Frame | One of the separate images used to make up a storyboard or film |
| Fx | Abbreviation for sound effects |
| Genre | A category of writing – for example, documentaries, sit-coms, soap operas, crime writing, romance, travel writing |
| Headlines | Text at the top of a story designed to catch our interest. They may be short, eye-catching, dramatic |
| Int/Ext | Abbreviations used in film and television to indicate whether a scene is interior or exterior |
| Masthead | The top section of a newspaper which gives the paper's title, price and date |
| Narrative | Story |
| OB | Outside broadcast |
| Panning | A camera angle used in filming: panning = moving the camera sideways across a scene |
| Phatic communication | Language used for social purpose rather than to communicate definite meanings – e.g. 'hello', 'hi', 'good morning' |
| Photojournalism | Use of photographs to record news events |
| Point of view | In filming, the use of a camera to show things from a character's viewpoint – e.g. imagine a scene with a cowboy walking into a saloon. We could show this from the point of view of the cowboy (camera moves into room and show people looking round) or the point of view of people in the saloon (camera shows cowboy walking in) |

| | |
|---|---|
| Press release | An information sheet sent out by companies and organisations to newspapers, television and radio news editors. The aim is to get the news team interested in covering the story |
| Pyramid story structure | Newspaper stories start with the main events. Then they give more details and eyewitness comments in short paragraphs. The paragraphs at the end of the story are less important than those at the beginning. This allows sub-editors to shorten stories by cutting paragraphs from the end |
| Pun | Wordplay, often used in newspaper headlines (e.g. a story about Blackpool called *We will Rock You*) |
| Readership | The group of people who read a particular newspaper |
| Screenplay | The script of a TV programme or film |
| Serial | Regular television or radio programme where one episode carries the story on from the previous episode (e.g. *EastEnders*) |
| Series | Programme with new stories in every episode (e.g. *Friends*) |
| Sit-com | Situation comedy: a comedy series built around a familiar group of characters in the same location (e.g. *Fawlty Towers*) |
| Soap opera | Television or radio drama that follows the lives of a group of people. The name comes from the fact that the first American soaps were sponsored by soap companies |
| Stereotyping | Making assumptions about a person based on the group they belong to – for example, assuming that someone wearing glasses studies harder than someone without. Advertising, in particular, uses stereotypes |
| Storyboards | A visual plan showing the storyline of a film in rough sketches |
| Sub-editor | Someone who gets a newspaper story into its final form – deciding the headline, correcting text, making any necessary cuts or changes |
| Symbol | An object which has meaning beyond itself – for example, a red nose symbolises the charity Comic Relief |
| Tabloid newspaper | Smaller newspapers aimed at a large audience. News is reported in less depth and emphasises human interest stories. The language level is lower, paragraphs and stories shorter, with more use of images. Content often includes more celebrities, media news and gossip<br>Examples: the *Sun*, the *Mail*, the *Mirror*, the *Express* |
| Target audience | The main group a media text is aimed at. It is usually defined by gender (male/female), age, and social class. There are different ways of classifying an audience. For example, a social grouping might divide people in this way:<br>Class 1 = solicitors, doctors<br>Class 2 = teachers and MPs<br>Class 3 = non-manual skilled workers (e.g. secretarial) and manual skilled (e.g. engineer)<br>Class 4 = manual workers<br>Class 5 = unskilled manual workers |
| Theme | Plot is what happens in a story. Theme is the issues the plot deals with. Themes might include crime, revenge, family life, and so on |
| Topic sentence | The first sentence (sometimes printed in bold, or capitals, or a larger font) aims to give you the whole story in one go: who, what, where, when, where, why? |
| Tracking | A camera angle used in filming: tracking = moving the camera to follow an actor |
| Trailers | Short films or soundtracks advertising a film or programme that will be shown later |
| Unique selling point | The key features of a product. Advertisers try to emphasise USPs to show that their product is different from their rivals' product |
| V/O | Voice over – the voice that tells a story or describes events over the top of a sequence of images |
| Zooming | A camera angle used in filming: zooming = moving the camera in for a close-up |

| Framework objectives | Unit and section reference |
|---|---|
| **Year 7** | |
| **Research and study skills** | |
| 3. compare and contrast the way information is presented in different forms, e.g. *web page, diagrams, prose* | 1.3, 1.4, 2.3, 3.1, 4.1, 4.3, 5.1, 6 |
| 5. appraise the value and relevance of information found and acknowledge sources. | 2.4, 3.2, 4.1, 4.3 |
| **Reading for meaning** | |
| 6. adopt active reading approaches to engage with and make sense of texts. e.g. *visualising, predicting, emphasising and relating to own experience.* | 3.3 |
| 7. identify the main points, processes or ideas in a text and how they are developed by the writer | 2.3 |
| 8. infer and deduce meanings using evidence in the text, identifying where and how meanings are implied | 6 |
| 10. identify how media texts are tailored to suit their audience, and how that audience responds to them, e.g. *popular websites* | 2.2, 3.2, 4.1, 4.2, 5.2, 6 |
| 11. recognise how print, sounds and still or moving images combine to create meaning | 1.1, 2.1, 5.1, 5.4 |
| **Imagine, explore, entertain** | |
| 7. use a range of narrative devices to involve the reader, e.g. *withholding information* | 1.4 |
| 8. experiment with the visual and sound effects of language, including the use of imagery, alliteration, rhythm, rhyme, etc | 2.2 |
| **Inform, explain, describe** | |
| 10. organise texts in ways appropriate to their content, e.g. *by chronology, priority, comparison,* and signpost this clearly to the reader | 3.2 |
| 11. select and present information using detail, example, diagramm and illustratoin as appropriate. | 3.1, 4.2 |
| **Speaking** | |
| *Pupils should be taught to:* | |
| 3. tailor the structure, vocabulary and delivery of a talk or presentation so that listeners can follow it. | 2.3 |

| Framework objectives | Unit and section reference |
|---|---|
| **Listening** | |
| 8. identify the main methods used by presenters to explain, persuade, amuse or argue a case, e.g. *emotive vocabulary, verbal humour* | 3.3 |
| **Understanding the author's craft** | |
| 13. identify, using appropriate terminology, the way writers of non-fictions match language and organisation to their intentions – e.g. *in campaign material.* | 2.3, 4.3, 5.4, 6 |
| 14. recognise how writers' language choices can enhance meaning: e.g. *repetition, emotive vocabulary, varied sentence structure* or *line length, sound effects.* | 1.3, 1.4, 2.3, 5.4 |
| **Persuade, argue, advise** | |
| 16. find and use different ways to validate an argument, e.g. *statistical advice, exemplification, testimony* | 3.1, 4.2, 4.3 |
| **Drama** | |
| 15. develop drama techniques to explore in role a variety of situations and texts or respond to stimuli | 3.2 |
| 17. extend their spoken repertoire by experimenting with language in different roles and dramatic contexts | 3.3 |
| 19. reflect on and evaluate their own presentations and those of others | 3.3 |

| Year 8 | |
|---|---|
| **Vocabulary** | |
| 7. review and develop their ability to: | |
| a) recognise links between words related by word families and roots | 2.1, |
| c) understand and explain exactly what words mean in particular contexts | 6 |
| 12. recognise how the degree of formality influences word choice | 3.2 |
| **Stylistic conventions of non-fiction** | |
| 9. adopt the stylistic conventions of the main non-fiction text types to fit different audiences and purposes, e.g. *advertisements, documentories, editorials.* | 1.4, 2.3 4.3, 6 |

| Framework objectives | Unit and section reference |
|---|---|
| **Standard English and language variation** | |
| 11. understand differences between key standard English and dialectal variations | 6 |
| 12. explore and use different degrees of formality in written and oral texts, e.g. *formal speeches, informal journals* | 3.2, 4.2, 6 |
| 13. recognise some of the differences in sentence structure, vocabulary and tone between a modern English text and a text from another historical period | 6 |
| **Research and study skills** | |
| 3. make notes in different ways, choosing a form which suits the purpose, e.g. *diagrammatic notes, taking notes during a video, abbreviating for speed and ease of retrieval* | 3.1 |
| **Reading for meaning** | |
| 8. investigate how meanings are changed when information is presented in different forms or transposed into different media | 1.4, 2.3, 3.3, 4.3, 5.1 |
| 6. recognise bias and objectivity, distinguishing facts from hypotheses, theories or opinions | 5.6 |
| **Imagine, explore, entertain** | |
| 7. experiment with different language choices to imply meaning and to establish the tone of the piece, e.g. *ironic, indignant* | 3.3, 4.2, 4.3, 5.4, 6 |
| **Speaking** | |
| 3. make a formal presentation in standard English, using appropriate rhetorical devices | 1.EA |
| 4. provide an explanation or a commentary which links words with actions or images, e.g. a *sports commentary or talking to a sequence of slides* | 1.2, 1.4, 3.2 |
| **Listening** | |
| 8. recognise the range of ways in which messages are conveyed, e.g. *tone, emphasis, status of speaker* | 3.2 |
| **Drama** | |
| 15. explore and develop ideas, issues and relationships through work in role | 3.2 |

| Framework objectives | Unit and section reference |
|---|---|
| **Year 9** | |
| **Spelling strategies** | |
| • applying knowledge of word compounds, origins, families and morphology | 2.1 |
| **Paragraphing and cohesion** | |
| 5. evaluate their ability to shape ideas rapidly into cohesive paragraphs | 4.3 |
| **Stylistic conventions of non-fiction** | |
| 7. analyse and exploit the stylistic conventions of the main text types, e.g. *parody* | 4.1, 5.4, 6 |
| 8. investigate the stylistic conventions of ICT, including CD-ROM, email, web pages etc | 3.3, 4.1, 4.2, 6 |
| **Research and study skills** | |
| 1. review and extend their own strategies for locating, appraising and extracting relevant information | 3.1, 4.1 |
| 2. synthesise information from a range of sources, shaping material to meet the reader's needs | 2.4, 3.2, 4.1 |
| 4. evaluate the relevance, reliability and validity of information available through print, ICT and other media sources | 1.3, 2.2 2.3, 3.3, 4.3, 5.4, 6 |
| **Reading for meaning** | |
| 6. comment on the authorial perspectives offered in texts on individuals, community and society in texts from different cultures | 1.1, 5.1 |
| 8. analyse how media texts influence and are influenced by readers, e.g. *interactive programmes, selection of news items* | 1.4, 2.2, 2.3, 3.2, 3.4, 4.2, 5.3, 6 |
| **Imagine, explore, entertain** | |
| 5. explore different ways of opening, structuring and ending narratives and experiment with narrative perspective, e.g. *multiple narration* | 1.3, 1.4, 2.3, 3.2, 3.3 |
| **Speaking** | |
| 2. use standard English to explain, explore or justify an area informal contexts | 1.EA, 3.2 |

# ACKNOWLEDGEMENTS

**The publishers gratefully acknowledge the following for permission to reproduce copyright material. Every effort has been made to trace copyright holders, but in some cases has proved impossible. The publishers would be happy to hear from any copyright holder that has not been acknowledged.**

'Road Signs' reproduced from the 'Highway code', produced by Highways Agency. Crown Copyright. Extract from *Aliens: Nightmare Asylum* Mark Verheiden and Den Baeauvais. "ALIENS"™ & © 2001, Twentieth Century Fox Film Corporation. All rights reserved. Used with permission. Extract from the script of *A Grand Day Out*, storyboard from *A Close Shave* and an extract from the Aardman website, www.aardman.com, reprinted with the kind permission of Aardman Animations Limited. Extract from *The Highwayman* by Alfred Noyes. Reprinted by permission of The Society of Authors as the Literary Representative of the Estate of Alfred Noyes. *Irn-Bru logo*. Reprinted with the kind permission of A. G. Barr plc. *Kellogg's logo*. Reprinted with the kind permission of Kellogg's. *McDonald's logo*. Reprinted with the kind permission of McDonald's. *BT logo*. The BT Corporate Mark is reproduced by the kind permission of British Telecommunications plc. Quote from 'Webpromotion Inc.' Reprinted with permission. *Crown Golf logo*. Reprinted with the kind permission of Crown Golf Properties LP. *Procter & Gamble logo*. Reprinted with the kind permission of Procter & Gamble. *MedNets logo*. Reprinted with the kind permission of MedNets. *North Systems logo*. Reprinted with the kind permission of North Systems. *Compaq logo*. Reprinted with the kind permission of Compaq Computer Limited. *M&M's material*. Reprinted with the kind permission of Abbott Mead Vickers BBDO Limited. *Interview with Derek Warren and 2 Barnardo's adverts*. Reprinted with the kind permission of Barnardo's. Four small extracts from 'The Times, 23rd July, 2000.' Copyright © Times Newspapers Limited, 23rd July, 2000. Reprinted with permission. *Plug and Play* by Dave Simpson, from The Guardian, 5th May, 2000. Copyright © Dave Simpson. Used with permission. *Weather forecast*. Reproduced with the kind permission of the Met Office. *Reports Local* from *Barmy* by Victoria Wood, published by Methuen in 1987. Reprinted with the kind permission of Methuen Publishing Limited. Extract from *Who Invented Television?* by Francis Wheen, published by Century. Used by permission of The Random House Group Limited. *Five Secrets for Web Design Success* by Renee Kennedy, found at www.greatpromote.com. Reprinted with the kind permission of Renee Kennedy. Page from the website of the Vegetarian Society  www.vegsoc.org. Reprinted with permission. Page from the website of the RNLI  www.rnli.org.uk/home.html.  Reprinted with permission. Page from the website of the Cats Protection League www.cats.org.uk/kitten.html. Reprinted with

permission. Page from the website of The British Heart Foundation www.bhf.org.uk. Reprinted with permission. Front Page from 'Le Figaro, 26 Juillet, 2000'. Reprinted with permission of Le Figaro – Syndication. Front Page from 'Al Hayat, 26 July, 2000'. Reprinted with permission of Al Hayat. Extract relating to Danny John, Executive Picture Editor at the Guardian. Reprinted with the kind permission of Danny John. Headline *113 dead in Concorde crash......* From The Guardian, 24th July, 2000. Copyright © The Guardian, 24th July, 2000. Used with permission. *MacDonald's Slappy Meal* by Adam Lee-Porter, in The Sun, 25th July, 2000.  Copyright © News International Newspapers Limited, 25th July, 2000. Used with permission. *Where's the ripcord?* By David Fisher from 'Metro' June 29th, 2000. Reprinted with permission of Atlantic Syndication Partners. *Voice of the Mirror – Going for Gold* extract from The Mirror, Opinion Column 25th July, 2000. Used with permission. *Baby in car seat survives 300ft fall down ravine* by Rosemary Behan, in The Daily Telegraph, 15th September, 1998. Copyright © The Telegraph Group Limited, 25th September, 1998. Used with permission. Extract from *The Faber Companion to 20th Century Popular Music* by Phil Hardy and Dave Laing, published by Faber and Faber Limited. Reprinted by permission of Faber and Faber Limited. Extract from *Q/Omnibus Press Rock n Roll Reader 1994*. Interview with Michael Jackson and Timothy White. Reprinted with the kind permission of Music Sales UK.

The publishers would like to thank the following for permission to reproduce photographs on the pages noted.

The Ronald Grant Archive pp.10, (*Braveheart poster*) 12, (*Casablanca poster*) 13, (*Godzilla poster*) 30, (*three Romeo and Juliet posters*); Aardman Animations Ltd pp.19, (*storyboard from A Close Shave*), 28, (*still from A Grand Day Out*); Redferns/David Farrell p.54, (*The Beatles*); Redferns/Michael Ochs Archive p.54, (*The Osmonds*); Redferns/Fotex/Olly p.54, (*Westlife*); Photodisc pp.57, (*four boys*), 88, (*single dolphin, two dolphins, several dolphins swimming,*), 100, (*mobile phone, brain scan, teenagers*); BBC Photograph Library pp.61, (*Blue Peter team, John Craven and Andy Crane*), 69, (*Richard Baker, Alastair Burnett, Angela Rippon, Moira Stewart, Peter Sissons*), 72, (*EastEnders*), 77, (*Children watching TV*); Mike Laye/corbis p.70, (*Victoria Wood*); Science and Society Picture Library/NMPFT/Hulton Getty p.76, (*Logie Baird*); Science & society Picture Library/DHA/NMPFT p.76, (*watching small TV*); Associated Press AP pp.98, (*Concorde in hanger, Concorde taking off, trail of fire*), 99, (*Crashed Concorde, aerial of damage*); Mark Wagner pp.98, (*Concorde on the ground*), 99, (*Concorde flying*); Corbis p.100, (*girl talking on mobile phone*); Gerard Lacz/FLPA p.88, (*pod of dolphins*). Action Plus/Glyn Kirk p.107, (*Tiger Woods*).